Your Wedding Speech
Made Easy

Also by J. Thomas Steele

Questions for Couples: What to Ask Before You Say "I Do:
A Primer for Planning Your Future Together and A Guide to
What to Expect From Premarital Counseling

The Bride's Guide to the Wedding Party: Choosing—and
Using—your Bridesmaids, Groomsmen, and Others to Make
YOUR Wedding a Success

The Tao of the Vow: The Path to YOUR Perfect Vows –
How to Write and Deliver YOUR Wedding Vows

YOUR Wedding Speech Made Easy: The "How-to" Guide
for The Couple (Writing and Delivering YOUR Perfect Wedding
Speech)

Your **Wedding Speech Made Easy:**

The "How-to" Guide for
The Father of the Bride,
the Best Man . . .
and Everyone Else!

(Writing and Delivering
YOUR Perfect Wedding Speech)

Book 4 of *The Wedding Series*

J. Thomas Steele

Disclaimer:

Front Cover Design by Neharra at Creativelog

ISBN- 13: 978-1534834729
ISBN- 10: 1534834729

First Edition

10 9 8 7 6 5 4 3 2 1

Dedication

To everyone who has to make a Wedding Speech:

Good Luck, Clear Voice, Proper Enunciation, and Damn the Butterflies!

and

To my late parents who showed me how a marriage should work. To my wonderful wife who shows me every day. To my son and daughter-in-law who inspired this effort. And to my daughter who may have a use for this book—though not too soon, I hope.

"Knowledge is of two kinds. We know a subject ourselves, or we know where we can find information upon it."

--Samuel Johnson (1709-1784) English writer, poet, essayist, and lexicographer

Dear Reader,

Thank you for choosing my book to "find information upon it." I wrote this book to be informative, helpful, and entertaining and trust you will find it so. Again, my sincere thanks for allowing me the honor of helping you write *your* Wedding Speech.

Best Wishes,

J. Thomas Steele

Table of Contents

Introduction

Whether you are a member of the Wedding Party, a family member or friend who has been asked to "say a little something," *or just in case you think you* might *be asked,* you have chosen the right book.

However, if you prefer to simply buy a few cheap wedding cards from a drug store and cobble their sentiments together into a speech, then this book *isn't* for you.

Speaking at such an important event as the wedding of a family member or friend is an honor and deserves both your attention and best effort. If you are unwilling to do that, then tell The Couple, "No thanks." But, you're not that kind of person, are you? I thought not! YOU are flattered that you've been asked to speak, and recognize that it is a privilege to do so! I recognize it too.

I sincerely appreciate your trusting me to show you how to create not just *a* Wedding Speech, but YOUR unique Wedding Speech. Before we start, though, let me warn you that there will be some work involved. Speeches do not write themselves, and while I know that this can be daunting and intimidating, it won't be all that difficult if you follow the information in this book.

A Wedding Speech is different from any other type of speech you may have given. It is as singular as the role you play in this wonderful event. Everyone at the wedding has some role to play but since you have been chosen to speak, *you* have a *very special* role to play.

YOUR Wedding Speech Made Easy is not so titled because of your role as a wedding speaker, but because you will learn how to inject YOUR distinctive personality into the speech and truly make the speech and its presentation uniquely *your own*. It offers not only information on personalization, but also information on preparation, motivation, and inspiration.

Speaking of presentation, public speaking may be the number one fear of adults, but it won't be a fear you need much worry about once you have read this book. Oh, you'll still get butterflies—even the most experienced performers of stage and screen do—but your butterflies *won't* become moths!

You will learn how to plan your remarks, organize them into a speech and deliver that speech, without embarrassing yourself *or* The Couple. Specifically, you'll learn how to prepare to write a wedding speech, how to actually write it, how to prepare to practice it, how to *effectively* practice it and how to make a wonderful and dramatic delivery. And not just create *a* wedding speech in general, but the particular aspects of YOUR distinctive wedding speech! *YOUR Wedding Speech Made Easy* is not just a title, it's a promise!

. . .

Although this book will help you with your wedding speech, the information in this book is also appropriate for speeches you may be asked to give at domestic partnerships, civil unions, commitment ceremonies, second (third?) marriages, and vow renewals. Moreover, the general information on speech writing and presentation is applicable for *any type of speech* you might give for school or business as well.

[To that end, I urge you to take notes and I have intentionally left plenty of "white space" for that purpose, including "notes" pages at the Appendices and the end of the book]

So, dear reader, *RELAX*! Read on and you will be able to give a great wedding speech, enjoy the reception, and celebrate the Love!

And remember: Love *is* Love—no matter *where, when* or *with whom* you find it!

Note: I'm certain that you will skip ahead and read *your* special section first (and that's okay), but it is important that you read the general sections on Preparing, Writing, Practicing and Delivering a wedding speech to understand how to create your speech. In fact, it's not a bad idea to read the entire book first. It's just possible that you may find something useful even in sections that don't seem to directly apply to you!

Also, in recognition of the many same-sex marriages that take place, I'll try as often as possible throughout this book to use the phrase "The Couple" where I can instead of "The Bride and Groom."

. . .

Portions of this book also appear in its companion, *YOUR Wedding Speech Made Easy: The "How-to" Guide for The Couple (Writing and Delivering YOUR Perfect Wedding Speech)*—A book you might recommend to the happy couple. After all, they have to give a wedding speech too!

Before We Get Started:
A Brief History of
Wedding Receptions and Toasts
(So you know what you're getting into!)

The Reception

Marriage, as we understand it today, has *always* been a celebration. Upon completion of whatever religious or civil ceremony was required to make the marriage official, the newlywed couple would *receive* their wedding guests (today's reception line), marking their first entrance (*their* reception) into society as husband and wife. Their family members and guests, representing the community at large, then celebrated the couple's *reception* into society.

This celebration included food, drink, and often music and dancing. Depending on the religious tradition, many weddings took place in the mornings and were celebrated

1

with a breakfast or if they took place at night, with a light meal.

The Bride's father usually hosted the wedding gathering and was the first to speak, having pride of place as he had paid for the event. Typically, he would thank the guests for their attendance since many had traveled some distance to be there, remark on the newlywed couple, and then publicly offer his blessings. His comments would always end in his encouraging everyone to raise a glass and drink to the health and happiness of The Couple: the wedding thus presenting them to the community as husband and wife and offering the first wedding toast of the celebration.

. . .

The Toast

The tradition of drinking *to* someone is a very old custom. It was part of the culture in the ancient world among the Greeks, Romans, Egyptians, Hebrews and many others.

The Ancient Greeks drank to their gods and begged favors of them by offering them a *libation*, a small portion of the drink intentionally spilled on the ground for them, which they offered in their religious rituals. It also became customary in non-religious circumstances to drink to the gods, to the health of the king (or whoever was in power) and to the friends who were gathered together.

This drink was most often wine, as grapes were considered a gift from the gods and were highly regarded as a symbol of the vitality of life. Thus, the wine made from them was also considered a gift from the gods. This gift, shared between the divine and mere mortal humankind, was certainly a celebration. Even today, wine is the usual celebratory drink for most social occasions, though beer or hard alcohol are also among the preferred beverages (except where religious custom dictates a soft drink). Champagne, a sparkling wine from the Champagne region of France, and made years before the monk, Dom Pérignon, received credit for its creation in the 1600s, is the wine of choice, by far.

However, the wine served at these early gatherings wasn't necessarily that appetizing. Wines were crudely made and made for everyday use; they weren't aged and cared for as they would be later on in history. Neither were they blended to create a uniform flavor, so various jugs might taste quite different from one another. Some believe that to mediate its acidity and sharpness many in the ancient world would place a piece of slightly charred bread at the bottom of the cup before the pour or float it atop the wine.

Often before the celebration would begin, a communal wine cup, what we would refer to as a "loving cup", would be passed among the guests for each to drink to whatever was proposed ("To the gods!", perhaps) and as each sipped from the same vessel they showed themselves united in celebration.

In other times, and certainly during the medieval period, when guests were more suspicious of poisons, a communal cup would offer some peace of mind—providing the host drank first!

However, it was usually impossible to offer such a thing at very large gatherings, so some scholars believe that guests would each "clink" their individual cups to intentionally spill some wine into each other's and so share the delights—or possible penalties—of the drink. This mutual sharing might be accompanied by the words "To your health!" (offered with either sincerity or sarcasm) and perhaps this is why that phrase is the most popular toast in most languages today.

Others, however, believe that the "clinking" was made to echo the sound of the bells used in some church services to chase away the demons and evil spirits from the gathering. Whichever supposition is true, we have been "clinking" ever since!

Note: Some believe it is probable that the use of wine at wedding receptions in the Christian tradition is a symbolic reference to Jesus' miracle at Cana at the wedding feast (turning jugs of water into wine). Others believe it is wholly unintentional, a holdover, perhaps, from the days of grapes (wine), being a gift from the Gods (or God). However, since many traditions blend over time, it's difficult to speculate.

So, why is it called 'a toast'?

If we've been drinking *to* someone and "clinking" for ages, when did *that* become "a toast?"

Though often done in ancient times, it was during the Elizabethan Age that it became increasingly common to add a small piece of burnt or spiced bread to a cup of wine or ale to improve its flavor. This small piece of bread had been toasted by the fire and was itself referred to as a piece of toast.

It's likely that drinking to offer health, good fortune or other best wishes to the same individual over several occasions was quite an honor and this popular person was then referred to as the "toast." This, perhaps, is where we get the phrase "the toast of the town" to describe someone who is well appreciated and in common renown.

As the quality of wine and ale improved, it was no longer necessary to float burnt bread atop a cup of drink, but the reference to drinking to another's health, goodwill or success remained. By the early 18th Century, the very act of drinking best wishes to someone was commonly referred to as a "toast."

However, history being history, there are many disagreements as to the origins of both the wedding reception and what we refer to as "toasts." History is awash with various supposition, speculation, and apocryphal stories.

Nevertheless, the *only* important history regarding wedding receptions and toasts is the history *you* will make with *your own* speech and toast!

The Unique Attributes of
a Wedding Speech

Every speech you have ever given has been unique. Perhaps the words of the speech were the exact same, but your presentation of them was different each time you gave it. The venue was probably different, and certainly, the audience and their reaction to you and your speech were different each time. In that regard, your speeches were not unlike a jazz performance!

In fact, it's certain that the speech you gave on the environment in your seventh-grade Science class was not the same speech you gave when speaking on the same topic in college. It's also a safe bet that the speech you gave in the lunchroom at work for your friend's retirement was different from the speech you gave to your bosses at the district business meeting.

My point is that though every speech has certain unique characteristics, speakers tend to forget these and believe that one speech is much like another. More often than not, they tend to believe, "I've given a speech before, and this one will be no different."

WRONG!

Just because you have given a speech before doesn't mean that your Wedding Speech will be a piece of (wedding) cake! Experience definitely helps, but a Wedding Speech presents some special challenges. So if you feel you already know what to do . . . *you probably don't!*

Moreover, if you haven't given a speech in a l-o-n-g time, or given just a few in your life, *don't worry*—you may actually have an advantage! Because of your natural qualms about writing and delivering the speech, you will probably read over the information in this book more carefully than someone else who is more certain of their abilities.

So, what makes a Wedding Speech unique and sets it apart from other speeches?

The Event—A Wedding Speech is given at a wedding event: at the rehearsal and/or reception. It is celebratory. The speakers each have a role to play at the event. The speech given is unique to The Couple whose wedding is being celebrated. As such, these speeches are usually one-off types. (Although, as you will learn, there are general rules and guidelines for each speaker's role that can be used any other time you have to give a Wedding Speech.)

The Content—The Wedding Speech is personalized; emotional; with a reliance on private information. There is usually very little research required. (I've done a lot of it for you; see the Appendices.) The speeches are short but powerful and memorable. It is a showpiece because it will most likely be video-graphed and is certain to be recorded on many audience members' mobile phones. In addition, it is possible that The Couple will have requested a copy of the written speeches to keep in their "Memory Box."

The Speakers—These people, of which *you* are one, have been personally selected by The Couple to "say a few words" at the event. This is an honor and *not* a chore! The speakers have a place of importance in the events of the day/evening and will have special duties to perform in their speeches. Though they are important, they *are not* the center of attention—it's The Couple (*duh!*). So for as wonderful as their speeches and the deliveries might be, the audience is theirs for only a few minutes (and that's a good thing!).

The Audience—Wedding rehearsals and receptions are closed ceremonies, so the audiences are special invitees, most often family and close friends. As the speakers are chosen from this select crowd, the audience is certainly friendly towards them. This is usually because the audience members are very happy that *they* don't have to speak and so are incredibly sympathetic towards those who do. Yet despite the number of people at the venue, the speaker's *real* audience consists of just *two people*: The Couple!

The Critique—There is none! There is no judgment, no grade given, and no one the speakers need impress (apart from The Couple). No matter how poorly the speech is written and/or delivered, each speaker receives, at least, a polite smattering of applause. (This definitely relates to the audience's sense of "there, but for the grace of God, go I!") However, by the time *you* read this book and follow the information in it, *your speech* *may well warrant a standing ovation*!

The Rehearsal Speech vs. the Reception Speech— Speakers may have to give both, but will give at least one of them. The Rehearsal Speech is more informal, emotional, looser, and more intimate than the Reception Speech. Reception speeches are usually more structured, having certain duties that each speaker must perform, and though still emotional, are often less so than the Rehearsal Speech. Though the Wedding Reception itself is not like a business get-together, a cocktail party, or corporate reception, it is like a business event in that it is an official celebration. The reception is a "good time" event, albeit a *structured* good time event. And unlike many business events, it is a very, *very* happy occasion.

The Venue—It may be a banquet hall, large ballroom, or a small room in the back of a restaurant, but wherever the event is held there will be certain things in common: tables, chairs, flowers, food and beverages (some alcoholic), and people. The guests won't be sitting in rows, like in an auditorium, but instead will be moving about, mingling with each other prior to the speeches. There might even be a little dancing before everyone sits down to eat and before the speakers speak. The speakers may be sitting at a long table, not unlike a dais, or could be in a cluster of tables near where The Couple sits. The speakers may have to stand up at their seat and deliver their speech or they may have to walk over to spotlighted stand microphone. If the venue is small enough, they may not even need a microphone.

. . .

These are just a few of the things that make a Wedding Speech very different from most speeches you may have given or probably will give in the future. It is unique in character and presents its own challenges.

But though it is certainly different, don't worry. Reading this book you will learn how to surmount each and every challenge and prepare for, write, practice and deliver *YOUR* perfect Wedding Speech!

Note: As you read on, I remind you that the process of writing and delivering a Wedding Speech is the same process you'd use for *any* speech you may have to give.

I urge you to understand the basics of the process so that this book will have value beyond the preparation for this one event, and I hope that you will take notes as appropriate. I've left both white space and note pages throughout the book for your convenience.

Reasonable Expectations

*"The only true failure is failing to learn
from the mistakes you make."*

I know that you're worried your words will fail you; afraid you won't come up with the perfect words or phrase, and concerned that your efforts will let down both yourself and The Couple. You worry that because you're not a professional speaker you can't possibly do this.

I also know you are nervous about writing and speaking, so I want you to understand something at the outset: neither your speech nor your presentation will be perfect.

"WHAT?" you may ask.

I don't mean to impugn your efforts or to discourage you, but rather to point out something you may have missed: *there simply is no such thing as perfection!*

Understanding that fact can be liberating if you truly understand that this or anything else you do in life will not be perfect, simply because it *can't be* absolutely perfect. Absolute perfection is an illusion!

13

Remove the scales from your eyes and note the illusion. Free yourself from the prison of perfection—a prison into which you have probably consigned yourself. Unlock your caged creativity! Set free your unbridled spirit!

Too poetic, huh?

Simply put: too many people get discouraged because what they do seems to them not to be "just good enough." Don't you be one of them!

As Voltaire translated the Italian aphorism, "The best is the enemy of the good." In other words, don't strive for "perfection" — if you truly do your best, it *should* be good enough.

When it comes to your wedding speech, if it *isn't* good enough, rewrite it. Keep at it—don't give up. But remember: good enough IS good enough, *just as long as it really is your best effort!*

If you expect absolute perfection, *you will be disappointed.* Accept that there will always be some nit-picky thing, some barely visible flaw, which will exist in just about everything you do—including this. Accept it and relish it because being human means being flawed.

Despite the time and effort you will put into preparing, writing, practicing and delivering your speech—or for that matter, anything else you do in life—there should be no reasonable expectation of absolute perfection. So don't expect what you do to be perfect. Allow yourself to fail, to have to try again. Why? Because here's a little secret: *failure often leads to success!*

Science and technology progress from failure. Artists and actors practice and fail before they create a masterpiece.

Did Albert Einstein immediately conceive the Theory of Relativity? *(No!)*

Did Thomas Edison immediately create a viable light bulb? *(No!)*

Did Mozart's symphonies immediately spill, fully formed, from his mind? *(Well, actually, it seems they did! Very few cross-outs and rewrites on his sheet music, unlike what you find on most other composer's manuscripts. Sorry; bad example.)*

But my point is this: read this book and do the work, and you *will* succeed in putting together and delivering a terrific speech.

If you have setbacks and become a little discouraged, don't worry—soldier on. Just promise yourself that you will give your best effort to be as *nearly perfect* as you can be. That is all anyone can—and should—expect from you.

However, if you allow yourself to be overly critical of your efforts, or you over-react to the well-meaning criticism and feedback of others, *you will not succeed.*

Accept any *reasonable* criticisms, from yourself and others; and accept them wholeheartedly and gratefully. *Learn from them.*

Stay positive! Don't sabotage yourself with worries that what you do isn't good enough. If you have the reasonable expectation that you will do well, *you will!*

Remember: Just do your best, but make certain that it IS your best. Put some work into it. And enjoy the work you put into it. Be proud of it. Speaking at a wedding *truly is a great honor.*

And, after all, I promised you *YOUR* perfect Wedding Speech, not <u>*THE*</u> perfect Wedding Speech!

The Rehearsal Speech

Before we begin the actual process of preparing for and writing, practicing, and delivering your *reception* speech, we need to address the *first* speech you may be asked to give: the rehearsal speech.

This speech is far less formal and much more emotional than the speech you will present at the reception. It is far easier to compose because this speech is rather unstructured, with many elements that you can ad-lib as you give the speech: you simply follow the flow of your emotions as you present it. Because of this, this general guide for rehearsal speeches is appropriate for *all* speakers invited to the rehearsal.

First, recognize that the rehearsal get-together is the party for the Wedding Party! It is solely for the participants, not the wedding guests. It is a smaller and more intimate event than the reception, and likewise, the speeches are "smaller" and more intimate. This is where the stories are far more personal (perhaps a little naughtier!) and much more emotional. This is the event where tears may flow freely, for here you are truly among family and friends.

Next, the only structure to this event is probably the order of speakers that The Couple has created. As to the speeches each person will give, that is up to the individual presenters. Remember, at the rehearsal, you are representing *yourself*, and **not** the role you play in the wedding! For example, at the rehearsal, The Bride's father is "Dad" and *not* the Father of the Bride. He can get up and tell a story and offer wishes that are nothing more than an honest expression of his love for his daughter—no formality, no duties to include; just a free-flowing, sincere, honest expression of your love, hope and best wishes for The Couple.

(However, it is always good form to thank whoever paid for the rehearsal—traditionally the Father/Parents of the Groom or whomever The Couple or MC acknowledged, *and* of course, to thank The Couple for inviting you to the event and allowing you to participate in the wedding.)

Writing this speech should require little real thought and no real research unless you choose to use a quote from the Appendices. Fifteen minutes of peace and quiet, a moment to reflect on your honest emotions about the wedding (*always* make them positive!), a treasured memory or two to share, and a sincere wish that acts as a toast to one or both of The Couple and you're halfway done. All you need to do then is write your thoughts down, read them over, create a few simple phrases to remind you of the more detailed portion of your speech and put these phrases on a note card or two—and that's pretty much it!

Share your speech with your spouse or a friend just to make certain that it sounds right, make any changes that you think are necessary, put the cards in the pocket of the jacket you will wear or the purse you will carry and *you are done!*

"*What?*" you ask, "No practice, no rehearsal for the rehearsal? Shouldn't I be a little more professional than that?" Well, *heck no!* (Okay, maybe a little.)

Remember, this speech is supposed to be rather unstructured and emotional. This speech is expected to be a little more spontaneous and, indeed, you are more than welcome to alter your planned speech as you hear others speak or as your own feelings and emotions come to the surface during the event. For a rehearsal speech, your note cards are merely a suggested guide, they aren't set in stone.

Besides, you'll give your "formal" speech at the reception, so for now, just relax and say a few heartfelt words and offer your best wishes. You do want to save the "good stuff" for the reception, don't you?

A portion of the rehearsal event usually has an "open mic" section at the end of the scheduled speeches where anyone attending may say a few words. Most of these speeches will obviously be extemporaneous and emotional, unrehearsed—and perhaps—unexpected. And that should be what your speech emulates: honest and seemingly off-the-cuff memories and emotions.

Even if you are just one of the "open mic" speakers, WRITE *something*. At least, have an outline or a few brief notes on a note card. Others will simply walk up and offer something off the top of their head or a pedestrian toast, but you'll stun everyone with your well-planned speech!

If everything goes right, then the entire rehearsal breakfast/luncheon/dinner should be filled with hugs, kisses, tears and honest emotion — that's what rehearsals are there for.

(Oh, yeah, and to rehearse the wedding ceremony!)

. . .

The basic guidelines for a Rehearsal Speech:

+ Introduce both yourself and your relationship to The Couple (family member, friend, school chum, etc.)

+ Speak as your *relationship* to The Couple dictates, not what role you play in the wedding; in other words, speak as a Dad, best friend, etc. NOT as the Father of the Bride, or Best Man.

+ Thank the host for the wonderful event you are attending and thank The Couple for allowing you the honor of participating in the rehearsal.

+ Offer a brief memory or two — something personal, emotional, humorous, sincere, whatever — as long as it comes from the heart.

+ Offer your sincere, best wishes and hopes for the both of them in the form of a toast to The Couple.

Again, these are the *basic* guidelines. You may add to them as you see fit.

Note: Please reference the Appendices for quotations and toasts that may be appropriate for your speech. And for information on using a microphone, see "Microphone Cheat Sheet" in the Appendices.

Preparing to Write *YOUR*
Wedding Speech

Thinking About Your *Wedding Reception* Speech

THIS is the big, formal speech. The guests expect to hear from only a few select people in the Wedding Party, and so The Couple asking *you* to speak is a very great honor indeed. Yet, many decline this honor. Most who decline believe that a wedding speech can be drudgery to write and intimidating to give. Others decline because they feel they are not up to the task. However, you are not like them—*you accepted* the invitation to speak, so as to any reservations *you* might have had . . . well, it's too late now! Besides, I am here to help.

It's time to prepare to write your Wedding Speech, and 'yes,' there will be some work involved. Oh, you could just stand up and "wing it" like many do at the rehearsal event, but you'd probably just make an ass of yourself and also embarrass The Couple. So commit to the work; keep reasonable expectations, and you'll see that it's really not that hard.

As with *any* new project, the first thing you MUST start with is a Positive Mental Attitude (PMA): A sincere belief that *you can do this*!!! [Grammarians: I used multiple exclamation points to emphasize being positive!!! (Oops, I did it again—with apologies to Britney Spears.)]

Not feeling very positive? Are you nervous about public speaking? Don't really know The Couple all that well? (If that's the case, you may have to fake your enthusiasm a little.) However, as you progress through this book and learn the tips and tricks, I'm certain you will gain confidence and become more enthusiastic—about the speech, if not The Couple. Besides, *reasonable* expectations, remember?

Whatever your doubts, you must set them aside and become excited about your project. The idea is to find a *positive aspect* to the work you will do and convince yourself that it is necessary—because it is! This is most likely the only time these two people will wed (at least be wed to each other) and it is certainly the only time so many of their family and friends will be gathered together.

Therefore, while I can understand your reluctance, giving a Wedding Speech truly *is* an honor; and one that you accepted: so buck-up, bucko! Any doubts you have will only make the task a labor, instead of the joy it should be. So suck it up; put on a smile (or, at least, fake it!) and let's get started.

.   .   .

The first step in the process is simply to think about what you might say as a representative of the role you play. Ask yourself: "Who the heck *are* you?"

Are you the Best Man? The Father of the Bride? The Maid/Matron of Honor? Perhaps you're one of the other members of the Wedding Party who have been asked to speak.

This is important to understand because who you are, that is to say, what role you've been assigned in the Wedding Party, will determine your duties as a speaker. Each member of the Wedding Party has a traditional role and duties to perform—unless The Couple has contacted you and told you otherwise. (Hey, it's their wedding, and they can set the rules!)

For the purposes of this book, the duties I refer to are those of the traditional speakers and I will outline what each speech by them should contain, but we'll get to that later.

Some expectations, though, are obvious: the Best Man will tell slightly off-color but good-natured stories about the Groom; the Father of the Bride will tell stories about "his little girl;" the Maid/Matron of Honor will tell stories about her friendship with the Bride, etcetera; and each and every speech will end with a sincere toast to The Couple.

In the following chapters, you will learn the general components of a Wedding Speech and then the specific things you must include based on *your* particular role.

But for now, all you simply need to do is *think about the role you play* and your relationship to, or with, one or both of The Couple.

Are you a member of the family, or a friend? A family member will have more memories to choose from than a friend of The Couple, but the friend may have shared special moments of which a family member is unaware. No matter who you are, as long as you write your speech from your own perspective, it will be unique and special. (_YOUR_ Wedding Speech, remember?)

These special memories will form a large part of the basic speech, as should any carefully chosen general anecdotes and quotes.

If you do not know The Couple that well, or have some reservation about either them _or_ the marriage, simply skip the "memory" part of the speech and use a more general anecdote and quote [see the Appendices]. Also, make your entire speech more general than specific. It will still be a wonderful speech for this special occasion

Lastly, all speeches should end with a toast to The Couple. Perhaps you have a favorite one. Perhaps you are stuck for one. Again, you can use the Appendices as a starting point.

. . .

In summation, to prepare for your Wedding Speech:

+   start with a positive attitude (PMA), and appreciate the honor you have been given;

+   know the role you play and its traditional duties (more to come);

+ think about your relationship with one or both members of The Couple;

+ note any special memories that might be appropriate for your speech;

+ consider researching and including other anecdotes and quotes; from the Appendices or elsewhere;

+ and consider what to say as a sincere toast to The Couple to end your speech

Writing *YOUR* Wedding Speech

All speeches, no matter the topic, follow the same basic three-act structure, as do most plays. Why? Because as in a play, a speech should be dramatic and the speaker should play a role, whether that role is a teacher, business leader or member of a Wedding Party.

The Greek philosopher Aristotle suggested this structure over two-thousand years ago. And just what is this remarkable three-act structure? It's a beginning, a middle and an end. (*Duh*!) Okay, there's much more to a drama's structure than that, but that's it in a nutshell; and if that seems obvious . . . it is!

The three "acts" for a speech are:

I. an <u>introduction</u> (to yourself and to the topic and your views on it);

II. a <u>body</u> (the longest part of the speech; this is where you make your point(s) and elaborate it [each one] arguing for or against it [each one]);

27

III. a <u>conclusion</u> (a final summation of your speech; a brief outline of the point(s) you made and a resolution to any question(s) you've proposed; also, you usually thank your audience for listening).

Simple! And appropriate for *any* speech you might give—in class, at a business meeting, at a convention, or elsewhere. However, it must be tailored for a Wedding Speech.

In general, I guess you could consider the "three acts" for a wedding speech to be:

I. Who you are and a Remembrance (a recollection)—a look back; possibly humorous, but always poignant and emotional;

II. A humorous story to act as a transition;

III. An Advisory (counseling)—a look forward, usually based on the speaker's experience, offering best wishes; it's always positive and contributes some advice

The Wedding Speech Template you will read about next provides only a *very basic* outline for a Wedding Speech. You must, of course, customize, elaborate and personalize it to make it your own, but I'll guide you through that when we get to your specific templates.

Please remember that the experience of creating your Wedding Speech will prepare you for *any* speech you might have to give in the future—like The Couple's anniversary or *your own anniversary!* So learning the "how-to's" of the speech (writing, practicing and delivering it) and its applicability elsewhere is a positive aspect beyond the specific scope of this book—see, this book *is* value for money!

As noted in the Preparation section, each member of the Wedding Party has certain functions (duties) as part of the speech he/she will give. For those of you who are members of the Wedding Party, there are individual chapters addressing the special issues specific to your role as a speaker.

If you are merely <u>a</u> speaker (*hey, that's still an honor!*), you can be less formal. For example, you have no special "thanks" to give; except to The Couple for inviting you!

Whoever you are, and whatever role you play: **Do not just write your random thoughts—write a *speech*!** Though The Couple may ask you for a copy of what you've *written* to keep and <u>read</u> later, you are writing a *speech*. What you put on paper is to be *spoken* at the rehearsal or reception, not copied and passed out for guests to read; and as you will discover, writing a speech is *very* different from just putting thoughts on paper.

Before you can actually put pen to paper (or fingers to keyboard), I ask you to read the next few chapters to understand a little more about what needs to be included in a basic wedding speech. And please note, I mentioned pen, papers, fingers, and keyboard. Nowhere did I mention hammer, chisel, and stone. Your speech is NOT carved in stone and should be edited—and edited OFTEN—as you get feedback! Remember what I said: do not expect absolute perfection! Simply do your very best and *you will* write a fine speech full of wit and advice, and told with eloquence.

Everyone's Wedding Speech
Template

This is a general outline to make you aware of the basic wedding speech format. *All* of the wedding speakers will follow this basic template. Later, you will find specialized templates for the specific role *you* play at the reception.

. . .

First, always gain the audience's attention and speak with a clear, strong voice

INTRODUCTION

Who you are (if you are not introduced)

Whom are you speaking about?
(the Bride; the Groom; both; or Someone else?)

Some short anecdote(s) (sincere, humorous)

Offer a short Quotation (if appropriate)

[See "Quotes" in Appendices]

BODY

A longer anecdote(s) (sincere, humorous)

A longer Quote (if appropriate)

[See Sample Speech Bodies and Quotes in Appendices]

CLOSING

Focus on seriousness; perhaps a piece of advice (a quote, or personal observation perhaps)

"Thank Yous"
(as appropriate, if not given earlier in your speech)

Sincere Best Wishes for The Couple
(if not included in Speech Body)

TOAST

(Serious or humorous, but *always* sincere)

[See sample "Toasts" in Appendices]

Now, think about *your* role as a speaker, then re-read the simple outline above. Think what *you* might say. Allow some time to find a favorite memory, to recollect a special moment, to research any anecdotes, song lyrics, poems or quotations you might consider appropriate — research on your own or use the Appendices in this book.

General Notes on Writing Your Wedding Speech

I know that you may feel that you are ready to begin writing your wedding speech—well, NOT JUST YET!

Please, read all the tips, tricks, hints and ideas for writing, practicing and delivering your speech before you actually begin to put pen to paper. Trust me; your patience will be rewarded—with thunderous applause from your audience; or at the very least, a sense of accomplishment.

Here are some general notes and interesting points to remember when you do write your speech:

+   The Couple should have already given you information about the length of your speech. If not, _ask!_ You don't want to be too brief or too long. On average, your speech should be 2–3 minutes _minimum_ and 8–10 minutes _maximum_. Five minutes

33

is darn near perfect! Most people deliver a speech at a rate of about 80 to 120 words a minute. And most people tend to speak faster when they are nervous, especially when delivering a speech because they hope that by speaking faster they can get it over with more quickly. But delivering a wedding speech requires a more deliberate pacing. Knowing the average rate of spoken words is between 80 and 120 words a minute, we can measure a speech in words. A three-minute speech could be between 240 to 360 words, a five-minute speech between 450 and 700 words, and a ten-minute speech between 800 and 1200 words. Of course, your rate may be different as you will try and follow your normal speaking cadence. But as you write your speech, keep the suggested time and word limits in mind. (The Wedding Speeches I have personally given run about 750 words and take about five minutes to present—not allowing for the roaring applause that always follows!)

+ Write as you would speak in a normal conversation. Perhaps choose a few more "ten dollar" words, but follow your regular patterns of speech as you write. You want your writing to read like a transcript of an informal conversation you might have, and to sound to your audience as spontaneous as possible. (And please note that sounding spontaneous takes time and work!)

+ If the MC or the previous speaker does not introduce you, you will need to introduce yourself. Most attendees will not know who you are, so always explain your relationship to The Couple. It should be something simple, like "Good evening. I am lucky enough to be (the Bride's, the Groom's) (father, mother, or position—Best Man, Maid of Honor, etc.)" You may or may not choose to give your name.

+ If you have to give an introduction to the next speaker after your toast, you say, "Ladies and Gentlemen, it is my honor/pleasure to introduce _(Name)_ , _Role_ ." Example: "Ladies and Gentlemen, it is my honor to introduce Robert, the Father of the Groom."

+ If you are not the mother or father of one of The Couple, then explain your relationship to the Bride or Groom: "I'm ____'s (friend, cousin etc.), and I've known him/her since the third grade . . ."

+ Everyone knows that you are not a professional speechwriter. Don't panic if you feel that you don't know what to say. Use the Appendices I have provided for you as a starting point for ideas and inspiration. You'll probably find all that you need there. The information in the "Speech Bodies" and the "Quotations" can substitute for or supplement your own memories as regards your particular speech template. If not, some quick online research may be all that you need.

+ Remember when I wrote before that one of the first things to do before you begin to write your speech was to *think* about The Couple? That was so that you could personalize your speech with your own recollections. Think about one, the other or the both of them. Surely, you have an appropriate memory. Often you will find that an *anecdote* is an *antidote* for an otherwise boring speech! Your brief account of a particular memory may be all you need. [Again, if you need supplementary material, refer to the "Speech Bodies" in the Appendices.]

+ If you do choose to include an anecdote or brief story, try and make it "universal" in nature; something that *all* your listeners can relate to. Chances are that most of the guests did *not* know the person as a child, or go to school or work with that person, so let your tale conclude with something everyone can understand. "I guess that means . . ." "The lesson here is . . ." Phrases such as these will let you summarize the point of your story and make it relatable.

+ Your stories and anecdotes should always be *positive* and *never embarrassing* to The Couple. Don't mention old flames! Don't mention the midnight skinny-dips during Spring Break at Daytona! Your stories or anecdotes should reflect your personal, *positive* relationship with the person or the both of them. Perhaps you can share a story about how they met, from your unique perspective; or how you've seen the person change because of their meeting the other. Keep the story about The Couple. Share *their* story. If you played a role in the story, underplay it. The Couple knows what you did and how important you are to them. It isn't necessary that everyone in the audience knows too.

+ A cute story is much more appreciated than a flat joke. However, if you do decide to use a joke, it should be easily understood and general in nature. Although you may have shared many funny moments with the person, try not to use "inside jokes" that will make the members of the audience feel left out.

+ Remember that your audience *wasn't* there if they "had to be there!" Remember too that there will be several generations in the audience so if your joke is too current you might lose the "older" crowd, and if your joke is too risqué, you'll be thought of as corrupting the kids that are there! Keep your humor appropriate to the occasion and the audience. You are writing to entertain, but not to *be* the entertainment!

+ Once again, use quotations and anecdotes to highlight your own story or the point you wish to express. Feel free to use the "Speech Bodies" and "Quotations" in the Appendices. In addition, you can always use your favorite poems, song lyrics, etc. to put your feelings into words. These sources are especially helpful if you *do not* know The Couple all that well. If you *do* know The Couple well, you might choose to incorporate short readings or quotes from parts of their favorite religious text, or choices of your own from your favorite text. However, it is always best to check with them first on this.

+ One question that always arises: should you use clichés? A cliché is simply an over-used and, therefore, too familiar word, phrase or quotation. However, that does NOT mean that it is inappropriate to use! It's up to you to either embrace or avoid them.

+ Keep your writing honest and sincere. Be natural. Be true to yourself. Let your writing reflect your personality. The listeners will get a sense of who you are and how you feel about this occasion from the words you write (*and* from the way you deliver them . . . but more on that later!). If you are naturally poetic or funny, include one of your own writings or observations. If not, rely on someone else's works. (Please consider the items in the Appendices.) Don't try to be someone you are not! Write honestly, sincerely, and from the heart.

+ When complimenting The Couple, use a few appropriate words (*this is why God created adjectives!*) or a brief story. But nothing too gushy or too long!

+ If you are a member of the Wedding Party, use the specific information in the appropriate section to say your particular "Thank Yous" (see your appropriate section—but not just yet!). This is probably the only formal and required part of your speech.

+ And whether you are or are not a member of the Wedding Party: always thank The Couple!

The Writing Process

You are not writing a book, so there is no need to explain the entire process of writing—as though anyone really can. For the three to five pages you *will* write, you'll follow a simple process: think, write, wait, read and revise, get objective input, revise, and relax.

Initial Drafts ("informal drafts"): As I mentioned before, the first thing you must do is <u>think about your role at the wedding</u>, as well as what you personally want to add. Once you have thought about what you might say, you <u>write it down to flesh out the basic outline for your role</u>. You add the names or titles of those you wish to thank; you add the memory or another story that you wish to use as an anecdote; you add the quote you want to use if you choose to use one, and so on. However, there may be some special circumstances concerning the wedding that possibly will cause you to rethink what you wish to say. Some of these are explained in the next chapter.

Remember: <u>Do Write; Don't Ramble</u>—tell your story as briefly as you can. <u>Once you are done and pleased with this initial effort—put it away</u>! Yep, just let it sit in a desk drawer for a few days. When you then re-read it, you'll do so with a more objective perspective. <u>You can then make any edits</u>. Chances are you will find this casual rewrite greatly improved the first one.

Feedback: When you are satisfied with what you have written, <u>allow someone else to read this draft and offer suggestions</u>. I know that it's scary to allow someone to see what you have written—but you need that second set of eyes. This person will most likely be a spouse or a close friend and they may be reluctant to point out problems or to question what you have written, but remind them that it's okay to be critical and to offer suggestions. Understand that when they do offer a criticism, you shouldn't be upset or take it personally. Remember, *you asked for feedback because you need it*, so when these "new eyes" criticize your speech—they are not criticizing <u>you</u>, just your words; and you want your speech to be as perfect as possible. So take the suggestions and begin to write a . . .

Second Draft ("formal draft"): "Once more unto the breach, dear friends, once more . . ." or if you don't like Shakespeare (*Hey, what's wrong with you?*), as they say in the vernacular, "Wash, Rinse, Repeat." In other words,

40

change and edit your first draft based on the constructive criticisms offered by your "second set of eyes." This time, your writing should be a truer reflection of what you intended to say, but you still must "rinse and repeat."

Final Feedback: And now for something new: *you* READ *them* the speech so that they hear the words coming from you. That's right, you read it *out loud*! Your "second set of eyes" becomes a "second set of ears." It will be a different experience for both you and your listener(s). Encourage additional feedback because the words as *heard* are often different from the words as read, so ask them for any suggestions.

Final Version: After having heard yourself say the words and having listened to your audience's reaction, you'll make any final tweaks necessary. As the name implies, THIS is now the best-written version of your speech.

Last, but not least: Be proud of yourself! (and *RELAX*)

YOU DID IT!

Theoretically.

You haven't really written anything without reading what's to follow, have you? Well, HAVE YOU? No? Okay then, Congratulations! And, please continue . . .

because you're not done yet. Soon you'll take these beautifully written sentiments and begin preparing them to present a speech.

For now, though, do as you did before and put your speech away and forget about it for a while. You deserve a day or two to relax. When you come back to it and re-read it with more objectivity, you may even want to make a few last edits before you begin to prepare your speech for practice.

NOTE: I remind you again that these are the basic steps you'd follow for *any* speech you might give at school or at work; just make a few minor changes and there you go! In addition, the chapters to come provide a wealth of detail on preparing and giving speeches—so you might as well learn them in case you have to use them in the future.

(It's just possible that this wedding speech will be so successful that you'll be asked to speak at other weddings! [Hey, anything's possible!])

Some Special Considerations

The Best Man Might Be a Woman!

I've attended a wedding where the only son in the family chose one of his three sisters to be his "Best Man." She was his best friend and confidant and so became his "Best Person" at the wedding. Unusual? Yes. Uncommon? Sure. *But, why not?* It's *his* wedding!

Today, many couples eschew the traditional titles and roles of participants in the Wedding Party. Sometimes it is a general statement of belief, a desire to break with tradition and create one of their own, or it might just be one of necessity.

What is important to note is that *whoever occupies the traditional positions still performs the traditional speaking duties.* Therefore, if you were the *"Man* of Honor" you would make the same basic speech as a "Maid or Matron of Honor." On the other hand, perhaps because of divorce or death, you might be a "Mother of the Bride" fulfilling the duties of the "Father of the Bride."

What is important to remember is that <u>your duties as a reception speaker are derived from the role you play and not from who you are (your relationship) to The Couple</u>! This is the very opposite of the rehearsal speech, which emphasizes your relationship to The Couple.

Thus, whatever role YOU play in the wedding will determine your basic duties as a speaker at the reception. These traditional roles for reception speakers are discussed later in the book. And if The Couple *has* decided on a different role for you, it is their responsibility to inform you.

Special Occasions

All weddings are special, but some are more special than others. Family dynamics and special circumstances may play a role in the wedding, and cause you to rewrite parts of your speech. Indeed, your speech might require a degree of diplomacy and sympathy. The following will provide you some information on writing for each of these extra-special occasions.

Second Marriages

A second marriage presents a situation caused by either divorce or the death of the original spouse. If this is the case, you may have to tread carefully when writing your speech, but The Couple should have told you already. It is their responsibility to inform you of anyone who should not be either mentioned or acknowledged in your speech.

Even if The Couple has given you no specific guidelines, use common sense and be careful—you do not want to stir up any unwanted emotions on this happy occasion. If you are in any doubt, *ask*!

Partners in a second marriage tend to be older. Certainly older than they were when they first got married. A few jokes about gray hair or a few wrinkles may or may not be acceptable. It's even possible that one or either of The Couple wants NO mention of their former marriage!

As a member of the Wedding Party, you are close enough to The Couple to ask them directly for any guidance. Even if you are *not* a member of the Party, you were chosen by The Couple to speak and they should have informed you of any specifics. Again, if in doubt, *ask*!

For a remarriage after divorce, it is common courtesy NOT to make sport of the first spouse. If the former spouse has been invited (and it does happen) and he/she sincerely wishes the best for his/her former partner and is willing to accept a good-natured jibe: *do not* give in to temptation! Even if that person has remained friendly with their former spouse, (especially likely if there were children) this is not the time to bring up memories of the first marriage.

For a remarriage after the death of a spouse, you don't have to say anything about him/her because usually, the surviving spouse will mention the departed in their speech. However, if that person was a relative or someone you were close to, it may appropriate to mention him/her *briefly* and reverently, but it is always best to get the okay of the surviving partner.

Some general neutral expressions for these occasions might be:

"I am happy that you found Love again."

"The definition of Love changes as you (grow older/go through life) and you are lucky to have found someone each step of the way."

"You are Loved again and lonely no more. I rejoice in your happiness as I hope you rejoice in each other."

"With age comes wisdom. And, since you are still young, (perhaps ad, "At least young at heart," if appropriate) I am glad to see you have wisdom beyond your years! _____ is a wonderful person and I am so happy you have found each other."

"It is said 'Age before Beauty', but with _____ you have found ageless beauty."

"Love keeps the heart young forever."

Absent Parents

Parents of one or both partners may be absent for any number of reasons. Most often, it is due to family politics, the result of divorce, financial or travel issues, age, poor health or death.

If the absence is due to family issues or divorce, ask The Couple if you are allowed to mention him/her. Do *not* assume you can. (Once again, they should have already informed you about this!)

If you are the Best Man, you have the duty of reading any messages or cards sent by any absent relatives or guests. As The Couple gives these to you, you can assume that they have removed any messages from relatives or others that they do *not* want to be mentioned; so you are safe to read any given to you.

As to a departed parent, if you personally knew this person it is usually appropriate to briefly mention them, by saying something such as "Your mother/father would be so very happy for you," or "I am sure he/she is looking down on you both and smiling." Anything more than a very brief statement and the happy occasion can turn maudlin.

Same-Sex Weddings

The Couple should have already informed you how they wish to be addressed. Many gay couples are offended by "Bride and Groom" and may prefer that you just use their first names, or terms like "life partners," "the Grooms," "the husbands," "the wives," "the Brides," "spouses," "companions" or simply, "The Couple."

It's also possible that they may also share some of the problems that have already been addressed—divorce,

47

family issues, the death of a former partner, or absent patents. If so, follow the advice already given; and if in any doubt as to whom to mention (or *not* mention): *Always Ask*! It's possible that, with everything else to do, The Couple forgot to mention their preferences.

A Special Note for Stepparents

Many parents today are stepparents. Perhaps you are one and have a "blended" family. Depending on the age of the child when you married, you have played a greater or lesser part in your stepchild's upbringing. No matter. Your child has asked you to the wedding and invited you to speak, so your stepchild views you as an important part of his/her life. Now *that's* love!

But what if their biological parent has been invited as well? And what if they too have been invited to speak? This can be an extremely awkward situation.

The Couple should have informed you if you are going to be the *only* parent asked to speak, or if they have decided to have, say, "Father<u>s</u> of the Bride," etc.

If the biological parent has been invited to attend but you are the *only* Father/Mother speaking, it is only right and courteous to introduce yourself as "the Bride's/Groom's step-father/mother" and to briefly acknowledge the biological parent and his/her contributions to raising the Bride/Groom. In your speech, <u>do not</u> refer to the Bride/Groom as "*my* daughter/*my* son" but use their name instead, such as "I remember when Jean was little . . ."

If using a quote that uses "daughter/son," you can always change the word to "girl/boy or child" or use the name of the person. Follow this rule too for any advice you might give to him/her in your speech. After that, you should proceed with the appropriate speech as suggested in this book. Remember, The Couple chose you for the role of Father of the Bride (etc.), so that is the role you must fulfill.

However, if the biological parent is *not* present but is held in high regard by your stepchild, ask if it is appropriate to use "daughter" or "son." Chances are that your stepchild realizes that you love her/him as your own. However, you do not want to have the Bride/Groom feel you are not acknowledging the other parent or, worse, feel that you are belittling that person as a father or mother. It is best to just ask your stepchild what they consider appropriate and accept any suggestions they make.

On the other hand, if The Couple has decided to have _both_ Fathers and/or both Mothers speaking, your role is greatly changed. The Couple should have explained exactly what that role will be. Perhaps they want you and the other parent to *each* offer a short speech and toast. Maybe they want both of you to rise and have one of you give a short speech, part of which will acknowledge and thank the efforts of the other; while that other speaker will then offer a toast from the both of you. Again, it is The Couple's duty to inform you of the format. Whichever it is, you would still introduce yourself as the stepparent and refrain from referring to your stepchild as "your" daughter/son.

However, whatever the circumstances, there is *absolutely no reason* why you cannot express your love for the child! On such an emotional day as this, that child—no matter how old she/he is—needs to understand how much they are loved—and loved by *both sets* of Mums and Dads!

Some phrases that you could incorporate into a speech include:

"I am honored to have been a part of raising (Bride's/Groom's name) and to have had (father's/mother's name) supporting me."

"They say that it takes a village to raise a child. In my case, I didn't have a village, but I did have the support and cooperation of (father's/mother's name). Thank you for being there for both (Bride's/Groom's name) *and* me!"

"Thank you for trusting me to raise (Bride's/Groom's name). And thank you for your support, and I hope I've done you proud!"

"Over the past ___ years I have watched (Bride's/Groom's name) grow..."

"I do consider you as my own child—if not of my flesh, certainly of my heart..."

"I hope you know I love you as though you were my own..."

Note: Many of the toasts and speech bodies in the appendices can be used for a stepparent's speech and, if giving a "joint" speech, changing "I" to "we" may suffice to make the toast or speech body correct to use.

.   .   .

Wedding planning is fraught with many details and it is possible that something you have thought about regarding a "special" situation may not have crossed The Couple's mind, so, as I have said before, *ask!*

Whatever they decide, it is always best to respect their wishes. You may not necessarily agree with them, but *it is* their wedding.

"Thanks" – giving

"Who Thanks Whom, and for What?"

As I mentioned in the general outline, certain speakers must include acknowledgments and "thank yous" depending on their role in the wedding. The following is a broad guideline. Specifics for each speaker will be included in a later chapter.

The usual "Thanks"- giving is as follows:

The **Father of the Bride**, in the English tradition, plays the role of host and sponsor of the reception, so he speaks first, and thanks *all* the guests for attending and offers the first toast to The Couple. In other traditions, he speaks last and *ends* the speeches by toasting The Couple.

(**Note**: Today the person(s) who actually paid for the reception performs these duties. It may be both sets of parents, the Father of the Groom, or even The Couple themselves. If this is the case, the Father of the Bride may be mostly a ceremonial role and, though he may be assigned to speak anywhere on the roster, he still usually speaks first or last.)

The **Best Man** thanks the Maid/Matron of Honor, even if the Groom has already done so because she is his counterpart. He also thanks the Bridesmaids on behalf of his Groomsmen. He always offers a toast "To the Bride!" but sometimes "To The Couple!"

The **Maid/Matron of Honor** thanks the Best Man and the Groomsmen. She offers the toast "To the Groom!" but sometimes "To The Couple!"

If the **Father of the Groom** is asked to speak, he welcomes his "new daughter" into the family and toasts her and his new in-laws, thanking them for raising such a wonderful woman. Likewise, the **Mother of the Groom** or **Mother of the Bride** would welcome their "new daughter/son."

If you are not one of the above, whoever you are and whatever role you play as speaker, (honored guest, Groomsman/Bridesmaid, etc.) what is most important to remember is that *you always want to thank The Couple* for inviting you to share this special moment and to offer them a personal, sincere toast offering your best wishes.

Preparing YOUR Speech
for Practice

Once you have finally written your draft and carefully crafted your speech so that it is both amusing and touching, worldly and intimate and expresses everything you wish to say, conveying your honest sentiments and sincere best wishes, {Wow! Job well done!] you now need to prepare it for practice.

+ If you have handwritten it on paper, NEATLY *print* it, <u>double-spaced</u>, on note cards if it is only a few paragraphs (which it shouldn't be), or on lined paper (if longer and hand-printed). Number the cards or pages in the upper right corner.

+ If you have entered it into a computer, set the font size to 14 or maybe even 16 and set the line spacing to <u>double space</u>, and then print it out. Handwrite the page numbers in the upper right corner on these first draft pages.

+ Why double-space it? The white space will make it easier to read each line and harder for you to lose your place, plus it gives you somewhere to write your Speaker's Symbols (more on these later) and make any final edits.

+ Finally, make sure you have left a wide margin at the bottom of the note card or page for any last minute notes you may make just before presenting your speech.

+ Remember, this is only a first draft of the speech you will practice! I know that you may have written it several times and it may seem ready for printing, but is it ready for *listening to*? Chances are you'll be revising it as you practice it, marking it with notes and ideas. If you have your speech on your computer, keep it in its own file; and for easy access, put the file on your desktop for easy access. Make it easy on yourself. Trust me, you'll be revising it several times.

With that done, your speech is ready to prepare for rehearsal.

• • •

Now that your words are printed on paper, you need to rehearse *speaking* them—after all, you wrote a *speech*! However good the writing *reads* on paper, what is important is how it *sounds* to your audience when the words are spoken. Remember: A treat for the eye may *not* be a treat for the ear!

Giving a wedding speech means not just saying the words but making a *present*ation; giving the speech as a *present* to The Couple—so why not make it as perfect a present as you can?

What you must do now is to turn your written words into a *dramatic* presentation.

"Wait a minute!" you protest. "I'm no actor! Heck, I was petrified of just reading the damned thing in front of a friend for practice! *What the hell!*"

Okay, you've vented. Feel better? Good. *Now relax!* Calm down. PMA, remember?

While your fellow speakers keep their heads down, staring at their speech, just reading the words aloud, making little or no eye contact, or expressing anything that might actually engage their audience, <u>you</u> won't be doing that.

<u>You</u> know that doing that is a disservice to the occasion and an affront to everyone there, especially The Couple. <u>You</u> know that you were invited to *speak* at the wedding, not to read. You know that—don't you? Of course you do! So I say, if you are going to speak, why not *perform* the speech!

Why not indeed? You have taken your time to carefully write words that reflect who you are (your personality) *and* your feelings about The Couple and their wedding (your emotional self). You want to deliver it as "spontaneously" as possible and have your effort recognized, stand out from the rest, and be a highpoint of the event—don't you?

Well then, your speech needs to not just be spoken but performed. And, as I said before, being spontaneous takes a lot of work, planning, and practice!

Now do not panic: it's really a simple procedure to make you an effective speaker and add some drama and panache to your presentation. All it takes is some practice, some feedback, and some more practice.

So read on and follow the guidelines presented here and you *will* deliver an exciting, "spontaneous" speech. Trust me, *you* can *do this*! Remember what Ralph Waldo Emerson said:

"All great speakers were bad speakers at first."
(*The Conduct of Life*, 1860)

. . .

Before you can practice your speech, you need to get your words *prepared* to be spoken, and you need to know how they sound aloud. Though you did this before when you were doing the Final Feedback stage of your draft, did you truly *listen* to the words you wrote as a member of your audience might? Probably not.

So read your speech *aloud*. Speak as you normally would. This time, listen to how you speak as well as to how your words sound and how your phrases flow.

How do they sound? How do *you* sound? Hint: If you have a Henry Kissinger-like monotone, you have *a lot* of work ahead of you!

If you feel that this is a chore, take a break and watch part of a movie. Seriously! However, don't watch the movie to take your mind off of the work ahead, but watch it to see how the actors perform the writer's lines.

As you watch, make note of how they evoke the spirit of the written word to convey emotional intensity in subtle or dramatic ways. I'll bet they make you forget that it's not them actually speaking; that all they are doing is taking the dead words on paper and bringing them to life through performance. They make the words sound like natural speech: easy, casual, and unforced—in other words, spontaneous. Yet they are only dramatizing words from a script—just as *you* will be doing when you give your Oscar-worthy presentation at the wedding reception!

When the film is over and you feel a little better prepared, *read your speech aloud again.* This time, as you read your words aloud, picture your favorite actors saying what *you* wrote. In your mind's ear listen to the way they might emphasize certain words or phrases; how they might add a pause for effect; how they might make a subtle gesture at a certain point for effective drama and emotion.

Remember, however, you are *not* your favorite actor. You are YOU! (*And if you are like me, you're neither as good looking nor as rich as your favorite actor.*)

You have your own unique enunciation, cadence, and rhythm. You will also naturally emphasize certain words and certain phrases of your speech. In addition, you will speak at a pace that is natural for you. These things are what identify "you as you" to your listeners when you speak. It isn't just the *sound* of your voice, but *how* you speak that distinguishes you. If you listen carefully to yourself, you'll hear it too.

Great advice, right—but how can you *listen* to yourself when you're concentrating on *speaking*? That's where modern technology comes in. I suggest that you record yourself on a digital recorder. Most mobile phones have a voice recorder application, so this should be easy to do.

By the way, when you play back your speech you may be startled at how your voice sounds in the recording, but don't be—everyone sounds "funny" when they listen to their recorded voice. No one is able to actually hear what they truly sound like to others. (*It has to do with the way our head and ears are constructed. You'd have to ask a scientist why it is. All I know is that it's just one of those things; like you can't lick your own elbow.*)

When you do listen to your recorded voice, be as objective as you can be.

+ Listen to *the way* you *say* the words and phrases you have written. Did the words sound okay?

+ Did the phrases flow? Or start. And stop.

+ Is there some drama in the way you spoke them? If so, did you like what you heard?

+ Could you hear the feeling? Did your speech pack an emotional wallop, or drop on your ears with a dull thud?

If you <u>couldn't</u> hear the feeling and emotion in your speech, keep on trying. Few people get *anything* right (or at least exactly the way they want it) the very first time.

And if it sounded really good, really dramatic and emotional . . . ? Listen again, but more objectively this time. Maybe it was a tad *too* dramatic and emotional. While your speech is meant to be sincere and a little dramatic, you are still an ordinary person and not a Shakespearean actor. Don't allow yourself to become *overly* dramatic as you read your speech, and please—don't go back and rewrite parts of your speech to add "purple prose" and flowery words to make you sound more "theatrical." It is always best to write your speech as though it were a transcription of any *everyday* conversation you might have.

As you read your speech aloud, allow yourself to emphasize what you consider the dramatic elements of your speech. After all, your *written* words convey your emotions, so why not let your *spoken* words convey them as well? Later, when you practice your speech in front of your spouse or a trusted friend, they'll help you recognize if you got the emotion right, need more or you've gone a little over the top.

If you still can't seem to muster the right emotion and drama, here's a little acting exercise: Try reading select sentences or phrases in *different ways* to explore how they might sound.

Start with this:

Practice saying the phrase, "I love you," and emphasize the word in italics.

First, say it as a <u>statement</u>: "*I* love you." "I *love* you." "I love *you.*"

Now try it as an <u>exclamation</u>: "*I* love you!" "I *love* you!" "I love *you!*"

And finally, as a <u>question</u>: "*I* love you?" "I *love* you?" "I love *you?*"

Wow! I'll bet you really heard the differences! A simple change in emphasis can change the meaning and emotion of your words and phrases. These subtle changes are the drama and the emotion that you will be able to convey to your listeners.

Now, re-read your speech aloud and try to bring that same drama and emotion to the select words or phrases that you have written. Then try reading your speech yet again with *different* emphases and listen for the differences. Decide just what kind of emphasis, and how much emphasis, to place on your phrasing to convey exactly what you want to say.

Everyone is different. Everyone has their individual interpretation of what phrasing sounds right to make written words mean what the speaker wants them to.

Frank Sinatra and Dean Martin could record the same song yet each made the phrasing special and the recording uniquely their own. (*Did I just date myself?*) So don't settle until the speech *sounds* right to YOU.

It's good to remember that even though you will be *performing* your speech, I know, you know, and the audience knows you are *not* an actor—but *everyone* is a little bit of a ham! It's human nature to want to show off a little; and, hey, that speech of yours *is* well written, so be proud of it!

Practice your presentation; let the drama flow so that your listeners, especially The Couple, understand that you have created a work of wonder by offering them as joyous and heartfelt a presentation as you can.

What the Heck are
Speaker's Symbols?

By now you have practiced your speech aloud, read it with "feeling" (and, I hope, not in a dreary monotone) and put a lot of yourself into it. If you pronounced the words, enunciated clearly, and emphasized the words or phrases you thought needed it, then you have created a dramatic presentation. Good for you! You'll do the same when you deliver the speech at the reception, right?

Probably not!

It is *very hard* to remember just how you practiced it. Plus, you'll most likely be a little flustered, maybe had a drink or two, heard the other speeches and toasts and you'll wonder if your speech is as good. (*That's really when you get those damned butterflies!*)

To help you deliver your perfect speech as perfectly as you practiced it you'll need to notate your speech with "speaker's marks (or symbols)" [sometimes called "emphasis marks"] that act as cues to remind you to pause, take a breath, make a mannerism, add feeling, etc. The more common ones, and the ones you will most likely use, are:

Pronunciation: If you do not know how to pronounce a word and look it up in a dictionary, you will see these marks. They help you understand whether the sound is a short or long sound, show accents and syllables, and stress or emphasis. If you do decide to use an unfamiliar word in your speech, copy the dictionary pronunciation! You do not want to mispronounce the word when you deliver your speech!

Ex: Pronunciation (pr*uh*-nuhn-see-**ey**-sh*uhn*)

Inflection: this indicates the rise or drop in the pitch of your voice when you pronounce the word. It is usually written as a slightly curved arrow and placed above the word. The arrow points **up** for a *rise* in pitch and **down** for a *drop* in pitch.

Ex: "What did you do˘?"

Emphasis: To emphasize the word(s) or phrase, underline it once for emphasis or twice for a particularly hard emphasis. If typing, you can use italics for single emphasis or underlined italics for double (hard) emphasis.

Ex: "<u>What</u> did you do?" "*What* did you *<u>do</u>*?"

Intonation: Like inflection, it means to add additional emotion or feeling to the word(s) or phrase by use of the tone of your voice. This symbol is usually a wavy line beside or under that part of your speech.

Ex: "I wish you both ≈Love!"

Pause or Stop: You probably use these symbols every time you write! The common symbol for pause is the comma (",") and for a stop, the period ("."). You can also use a single diagonal line ("/") for a common pause or a double diagonal ("//") for a longer pause. Use an ellipsis (". . .") for an emphasized longer pause. For a full stop, there is nothing better than the good old period—PERIOD!

Ex: "I'm not sure what will happen, but // I'm ready for it."

"I'm not sure what will happen . . . but I'm ready for it."

Pause to Take a Breath: Please remember to breathe when you speak! That would seem obvious, but some speakers tend to take a deep breath before they begin and then forget to breathe as they speak. To be sure you remind yourself to pause for a breath, use the bracket symbols with a capital B between them ("[B]"). It is common to take a short breath between paragraphs.

Mannerisms: If your speech requires you to gesture for either a particular emphasis or to make a point, you can use the parentheses with a capital G (for Gesture) between them ("(G)"). Of course, you have to remember *what* gesture you have to make!

To be certain that you have notated correctly, record your speech and playback your presentation. Carefully listen to it. If you followed the symbols you have included in your writing, you should have recreated the same drama and emotion that you did a few minutes before. Make any final changes you need to in your notations, record it again and listen to your presentation. You have just prepared a speech you can repeat again and again!

Maybe.

. . .

Now that you have initially notated your speech with the Speakers Symbols, and you think it's right, read your speech in front of someone you trust for feedback. Remind them, indeed encourage them, to be critical of your presentation. But remind them that they are <u>not</u> to critique your performance or your actual delivery. Instead, they are to listen to *the way the words are spoken* and the dramatic emphasis and emotion they *hear*—not the presentation and performance they *see*! In fact, you could have them listen with their eyes closed or just play them a recording of your speech.

(Note: You may also want *this same person* to watch you practice your delivery later on so that they can compare the aural presentation [the way it's heard] and the visual presentation [the way it's seen]. That way, they will already be familiar with both you and what you need them to do.)

It is very important that you get this feedback so that your presentation of the words will both emotionally involve and affect the audience, especially The Couple. Perhaps what *you* thought was fine, your listener considers heavy-handed. Accept any criticism given and don't allow yourself to become discouraged. Think back to your movie and imagine how many times the director asked your favorite actors to "do it again" because it "just didn't sound right."

However, if you feel strongly that *how* you said it *is* the right way to say it, leave it alone! After all, these are *your* words and they are an expression of *you* as an individual. Therefore, if your presentation of them is a true reflection of who you are, say them as you will! After all, you have to be honest with yourself, to be honest with your audience! (It's *YOUR* Wedding Speech, remember?)

When you have read and reread your speech aloud, noted your own and others feedback so that you have all of your speech notated just the way you want it, and verified that your speaker's marks are entered at the correct spots, *then* you can begin practicing your speech. Your delivery will continue to improve and your words will come even more alive as you do so.

It is important to remember, though, that the speaker's marks are merely reminders of how you wish to say certain parts of your speech. Just because your speech is notated, don't think that you can just fold it up, put it in your pocket or purse, whip it out at the reception, and deliver the same speech you did right now. PLEASE do not allow yourself to think that your notations end the need for practice!

I know that this sounds like a lot of work, but the drama and emotion you have infused in your speech *will be* appreciated by everyone there; especially The Couple. So, practice your presentation because the old adage is very true: "People don't often remember *what* you *said*, but they always remember how you made them *feel*."

Note: You may look at your notated speech and think that it "looks funny" and that the rules of punctuation have gone crazy. They have. Remember, you have notated your *writing* for *speaking* and so you may have commas, periods, etc. where they might not necessarily belong.

Practicing YOUR Speech

(And Learning How to Fight the Dreaded Butterflies!)

You have been diligent in following the guidelines in this book so far (*haven't you?*), so make your practice all the more effective by following the suggestions here. After all, you've committed to this, put in a lot of work writing your speech and preparing it for practice, so why not make its eventual delivery at the reception as faultless as possible? Yet, practice is the thing that many wedding speakers fail to do.

Oh, maybe they'll practice a couple of times, then get discouraged and stop; or they let their nervousness get the best of them (those damned butterflies!); or they let themselves think that they don't need to practice, that everything will be okay because their speech is all marked up with Speakers Symbols, no way to mess it up, right? So they quit. Just stop preparing.

Well, *Don't <u>YOU</u> do it!*

Don't give up after a failed first attempt or allow yourself to become discouraged or wallow in failure. Remember what I said before, "Failure often leads to success." Just keep trying! After all, you had to rewrite your speech several times before you got it just the way you wanted it, didn't you? It will be the same when you practice your presentation.

And think back to when you were a kid—I'll bet you fell off both your bike and your roller skates when you were first learning how to use them. But what happened? You kept at it and mastered them! As an adult, you've done the same at your job and other pursuits when you had something new and challenging to learn—eventually, you mastered it too.

That old chestnut: "A visitor to New York City stops a man on the street and asks, 'How do you get to Carnegie Hall?' The man replies, 'Practice, practice, practice!'" is more than appropriate. You will master nothing, gain no self-confidence and probably embarrass both yourself and The Couple unless YOU "practice, practice, practice!"

There are many things to practice for the proper delivery of your speech. Obviously, you want to present your words in an emotional and dramatic fashion, and you have used your Speaker's Symbols to help accomplish that, so now we must turn our attention to the mechanics of your presentation. In the following pages, you will learn about practicing projection, posture, eye contact and breathing. I will address things that might seem scary at first, but persevere: YOU CAN DO THIS! (PMA)

In fact, let that be your mantra throughout this whole experience. Close your eyes, take a deep breath, inhaling through your nose, and s-l-o-w-l-y exhaling through your mouth, and mentally repeat your mantra—"You CAN do this!" Or choose whatever mantra you like, as long as it is positive and affirmative. Truth be told, self-affirmation really works. We all seek validation for our efforts. Usually, we seek it from others but why not validate our own efforts?

C'mon, you have written a killer speech and gotten feedback on how best to present it with a modicum of drama and sincerity, so why not practice your delivery to ensure the effect of all the work you have put into it?

Please believe me, the drama and emotion you have infused in your speech *will be* appreciated by the attendees. As I wrote before: "People don't often remember *what* you *said*, but they always remember how you made them *feel*," and they will be grateful for it.

Besides, you gotta learn how to fight those butterflies!

Practice, Practice, Practice

Chances are you will be practicing your speech at home, in a safe and friendly environment. You may feel a little self-conscious rehearsing your speech aloud, but that is nothing to worry about. The more you practice, the more self-confidence you'll gain.

71

But, no matter how confident you eventually become, on the day you actually give your wedding speech, as you stand before The Couple and assembled guests, you *WILL* be nervous!

In the following chapters on delivering your speech, you'll learn some tips and techniques for fighting your fears; but for now, here are some pointers on how to cope with them.

. . .

<u>Learn to accept that you will have some anxiety</u>. Everyone gets the butterflies!

Your goal is to learn how to keep them mere butterflies and not let them turn into moths.

So how do you overcome your nerves? Understand what is happening and you can develop a Positive Mental Attitude (PMA) about it.

First, <u>stay calm and *Don't Worry* about it</u>! I know that that is easier said than done, but remember: the more you worry and fret about it, the more ingrained that worry becomes—and the bigger the "fear monster" grows. You ARE going to be a little nervous; most professional speakers and actors get nervous before *they* speak. Just accept it; in fact, *own it*! Besides, it ain't all bad—a little nervousness will help you focus. And you know what? As with many things, once you "get rolling" with your speech you'll find it becomes easier!

Second, you need to gain confidence, and one way to do it is to keep everything in perspective.

While it's true your speech is an *important* part of the reception, it is only *a part* of the reception! It's just a speech. A few minutes of your life, that's all it is! Its importance rests in the memory of those assembled. So as long as you have confidence in yourself, you'll *show* confidence; your voice will proclaim it and that is what everyone will see and hear as you speak! They'll hear your speech but they'll *feel* your words and though they'll most likely forget the words themselves, they will remember that feeling!

Third, remember that you have spent a great deal of time preparing your speech, so you need to spend time practicing it. Don't ignore the hard work you've already put into your speech. In fact, you should be proud of it!

Know this: *Even if practice doesn't make it perfect, it makes it better than it was!* ("better-er" as my little daughter used to say. So, practice and *you will* become "better-er!")

Okay, feel a little more at ease? Then grab a copy of your notated speech and let's get to work!

. . .

And work it is! You may want to write down your speech several times, saying each word to yourself as you do so. Your copying out the speech will help you memorize it.

"Say WHAT? Didn't you say NOT to memorize it?"

Yes, I did, and you *shouldn't* try to memorize your *entire* speech. As I said, don't *try* to memorize *everything*! If you do, and you lose your place when you deliver it, chances are you'll panic and your mind will go blank; so don't allow this to potentially ruin your moment at the reception. But . . . the repetitive task of recopying your speech and pronouncing each word as you do so *will* help imprint the phrases you wrote and make your speech sound more natural than it would sound if you just blankly read the words. You need to look up from your writing and look out into your audience. You will certainly lose audience sympathy if you have your head buried in your notes, just reading what you wrote, no matter how effective you think your Speakers Symbols are.

Don't think copying your speech will work? Well then, why did your first and second-grade teachers make you copy your spelling words 25 times each, repeating each word every time you did so? Could it be that you actually *remembered* them when you were done? Think back—it worked! You know you learned those spelling words!

Your wedding speech is only a few hundred words, so it's not like you are copying and recopying a hundred page manifesto! C'mon, just *do* it—don't wimp out!

As you become more familiar with your speech, you can now <u>outline the key phrases</u> and these will help you remember what you have already "memorized." Simply take a highlighter and highlight the key phrases, (always copy any Speakers Symbols you have noted) to your note cards/papers. The cards/papers will be there to keep your speech on track and in order as you speak. Remember, though, that they are just helpers, meant to serve as a crutch.

When practicing your speech, you should use these shortened, annotated cards/pages; and as you become increasingly confident in your performance, you might consider using them for giving an extemporaneous speech. (If you would rather, you can keep a copy of your *full speech* with you as well. Kinda like a *uber*-crutch.)

Note: The only thing you should actually *try* to memorize is your toast. That way you can make eye contact with the person(s), usually The Couple, to whom you are speaking.

. . .

You must practice! Practice you must! When I wrote about reading your speech aloud, do you remember what I said about imagining your favorite actors doing so?

Now it is time for you to imagine them rehearsing their part and saying *your* lines over and over—and you need to do the same. Remember, any speech you have *ever given* had to be practiced to help you gain the confidence to present it properly and to create the right impression on your audience. Whether that speech was a book report in fifth grade or the annual report you presented before your company's CEO—practice made it "better-er."

Some "real life" things to consider for proper practice:

+ Worried you don't have the time to practice? Don't worry—you'll *find the time* to practice your speech. This isn't as though some irrational personal trainer has demanded you follow an intricate physical exercise regimen—it's only a speech of a few minutes duration. Take a good look at your schedule; you'll find the time to practice, trust me. *(My sincere hope is that you aren't winded practicing your speech or you just* might need *a personal trainer!*)

+ Just how long should it take to practice your presentation? Since The Couple has already given you a suggested time limit for your speech and you have condensed your speech onto those few note cards/papers, it should probably only take 15 minutes *max* to practice delivering the speech—so, no biggie! There really is no excuse *not* to practice. Just rehearse your speech a once a day (twice a day if possible).

+ Just like the exercise regimen I mentioned before, <u>the more you practice your presentation, the stronger your "speaker's muscles" will grow; the more self-confidence you will gain, and the more positive you will feel about giving your speech.</u>

+ Remember PMA (Positive Mental Attitude)? The more positive you are about your practice and the more practice you do, the more proficient you will become. And while there may be no such thing as perfection, proficiency will get you extremely close to it!

+ <u>Stand tall!</u> Not just metaphorically, but actually. Slumped shoulders and a shy stance will ruin your presentation. <u>So practice your posture as you practice your speech.</u>

+ As you practice *saying* your speech, remember that <u>the natural anxiety you will feel at the event will cause you to either speak *veryrapidly* or v-e-r-y s-l-o-w-l-y.</u>

+ Chances are you will feel this stress even though you are only practicing your speech! Try and relax, and <u>maintain your natural speaking pace</u>. Practice maintaining this pace. The more natural your pace becomes, the easier it will be to repeat that pace when you finally deliver your speech.

+ Also, <u>know that at the event you might feel the need to speak *L O U D E R*</u>. When people become anxious they also tend to feel the need to speak louder. While you must certainly project your voice loud enough to be heard, you should not speak so loud that it seems you are shouting your speech. Speak only as loud as you need to. (If you have a chance to visit the venue before the reception, you can have a friend stand towards the back of the room and you can have him/her signal when they can clearly hear you. Just remember the approximate loudness and you are all set.)

+ <u>If you are using a microphone, and you probably will, remember to speak *normally*</u>. The microphone will amplify your voice, so you do not to speak loudly. Simply speak as you normally would and keep a well-modulated voice. By the way, if you know you will be using a microphone, practice using one by holding a hairbrush or spoon when you practice your speech. I know it sounds juvenile, but it helps. (See the microphone tip sheet in the Appendices)

+ Don't forget to pause to breathe during your speech! You may have already notated pauses for breaths on your speech, but if you haven't, remember to pause between each paragraph. If you *have* notated pauses for dramatic effect, use these to take a breath. Inhale slowly and exhale slowly. It only takes a second or two to catch your breath! The pauses not only help you relax a moment but will also help give you the power to project your voice and enunciate more clearly. Plus, you won't sound winded or suddenly have to gasp for breath during your presentation.

The more you practice your speech, knowing what you now know, the better you will be able to cope with any problems concerning posture, pace, projection, and breathing.

. . .

+ For the ultimate practice of your delivery: *Practice in front of a mirror*! Did you know that's what many performers do? Watch yourself in a mirror to see what you look like as you speak. After all, this is what your audience sees, so don't be afraid to look at yourself performing your speech.

+ When it comes to practice, remember what I said before: Don't be a slouch! Literally. Posture is important—it a sign of either confidence or fear. Are you standing straight and confident or are your shoulders hunched in defeat? And your face betrays your emotions even more! Are you smiling?—after all, this *is* a happy occasion! Do you look sincere?—this *is also* a solemn occasion! Do you appear relaxed, yet confident? Do your gestures, if any, look natural or exaggerated? Just what *does* your body language say about you?

+ Also, practice glancing left and right as you should when you address the audience. Eye contact is very important to help you engage the audience's attention. Remember in school, even if the teacher was boring, the minute he or she made eye contact with you, you felt a little more obligated to pay attention to what was being said. Same "hear" (pun intended). The only difference is that *your* speech will be exceptional!

+ Continue to rehearse in front of a mirror until you have gained enough confidence to practice in front of a friend or partner. He or she will probably be the same person who listened to you when you practiced before, so you should already feel confident practicing your speech in front of them. Whoever your practice audience is, remind this person to give you honest feedback. Allow them to be critical. After all, you are practicing for a one-time-only performance, so you need all the pre-performance feedback you can get!

+ <u>Encourage them to *watch* you and *not just listen* to your words!</u> You are now practicing your *total* performance (words, dramatic emphasis, and delivery) and no honest criticism should be unwelcome.

+ <u>And if you are *really* serious about delivering a perfect speech, ask your friend(s) to record you on their mobile phones or with a video camera.</u> I know it was hard enough to listen to yourself on the voice recording when you first practiced reading your speech aloud or watching yourself in a mirror, so I can imagine your fear at watching yourself on video! However, don't be afraid to watch yourself: chances are you'll be video-graphed at the reception anyway, so might as well see what you'll look like. This will give you a "heads up" to correct any flaws that you might notice in your presentation, such as slouching, too many gestures, etc.

+ As I already mentioned, <u>if you think that you will be using a microphone,</u> practice your speech holding a hairbrush or spoon and speaking into it. Just like you probably did when you were 10 years old and wanted to be a rock star! See the Appendices for microphone tips.

. . .

All of the information above is only a list of things that *need to be* practiced. *It is up to you to actually practice them!* **Make the commitment.**

I have written the above assuming that you do indeed have the confidence to practice in front of a person. Maybe you already have that confidence, maybe you don't. I do know that quite often the confidence one feels with one person or a small group can disappear when you have to speak in front of a crowd. To that end, let me talk a little about fighting the Fear Monster . . . and those damned butterflies!

Butterflies, Moths and the Fear of Public Speaking

Although practice will help you gain confidence, let's face it: you are probably *terrified* of getting up in front of an audience and speaking to them, *right*?

Well, you are not alone! If there really is strength in numbers, you're one of a vast army of *glossophobics*— people with a fear of public speaking. In fact, for many adults, the fear of death is their *second* greatest fear!

But just what is it that people are afraid of?

What scares the living daylights out of most people isn't standing there and *presenting* what's been written; no, indeed, they think their speech is great! What most people fear is that *their audience* won't think that it's great.

What most people fear when speaking in public is:

~ Public humiliation

81

~ Embarrassment

~ Ridicule

~ Not being accepted by the audience they seek to please

~ Being in the spotlight—the center of attention—seen by all, and seen to be alone and vulnerable

~ Opening up ones-self to a group of strangers

And

~ general social anxiety!

Whoa!

In a few words: it's not so much a fear of being uncomfortable or of potential failure, as it is a fear of *everyone* <u>*noticing*</u> *how uncomfortable you are and/or that you might fail!*

So, what can *you* do to get over or, at least, mitigate the fear?

<u>First, you have to acknowledge it.</u> Fear is a natural, human response to an unfamiliar or threatening situation. Own up to it; admit you will be afraid or, at least, a little nervous. Stare fear right in the face! In fact, don't just face it: face it down! Look it square in the eyes, understand what it is and *laugh at it!* It's a joke! It can't hurt you— unless *you* let it! Only *you* can hurt *you* and that ain't gonna happen! Why? Because you'll know what to do to defeat that rascal! Adding my own two-cents to a paraphrase of

Franklin Delano Roosevelt's famous quote, "The only thing you have to fear is fear itself and the worry that you will not be able to control your reaction to it." (But you *can* learn how to control it or, at least, tamp it down, as you'll see.)

So what is fear, itself? Many view fear as an acronym for **F**alse **E**vidence **A**ppearing **R**eal. And that's a pretty good summation.

<u>When it comes to public speaking, fear is an illusion your mind creates</u>! Fear exists whenever you challenge the unknown and create self-doubt. You're an everyday person, not a professional speaker, so you burden yourself with these nagging questions: *Will my speech be any good? Will I do a good job delivering it? Will the audience like me? Will I disappoint The Couple?*

The more you worry and doubt, the more your body reacts. The more your body reacts, the more you worry. That's one *helluva* vicious circle!

<u>It's all about perception</u>! Sweaty palms may be your body's natural reaction, but it all starts in your mind (as you will see). And since your mind and body feed each other in a symbiotic relationship, your fear increases. Your anxiety is produced by your perceptions; so, for example, your palms sweat, you see your palms sweat, and your anxiety grows, which makes your palms sweat even more.

See, the vicious circle *is* all about perception! Fear's only reality is what *you* give it, so let it fade away! Because: [*Grammarians, please look the other way*!] <u>*You are NOT going to let you hurt you*</u>!

<u>The best way you can send fear on its way is by doing just what you have already begun to do: prepare, practice, and then practice some more.</u>

Yep, that's pretty much it—

<u>Practice = Proficiency = Confidence = Comfort!</u>

If you feel familiar with your speech and comfortable with your presentation of it, you are half-way there. Now that's not to say you won't be a little nervous when you begin to present your speech. "Speechifying'" isn't your wheel-house; your forte; what you normally do. This is an *un*natural situation, so it's only natural to be a little nervous, and your body will naturally react to that nervousness. However, since you don't give public presentations for a living, (*if you did, you'd be writing a book about giving speeches instead of reading mine*) you don't even need to kill the fear monster—just shrink it down to a manageable size and let its hold over you slacken!

.   .   .

And what exactly is the Fear Monster doing to your body and how can you reduce its grip? Here's a look at what happens so you'll know what exactly *will* happen. This way you'll be aware of it and less panicked when it *does* happen.

In your situation, addressing a group of relative strangers (*or strange relatives as the case may be!*) you'll experience an anxiety that is known as "fight or flight." In other words, do you stand your ground or run away?

In this situation your brain sends a signal for the release of adrenaline which will affect you by causing your blood pressure to rise, your palms and forehead to sweat, your mouth to feel dry, your pupils to dilate, your voice to quiver, your breathing to become more rapid (hyperventilation) to pump up your blood with oxygen. AND your hands to shake, your muscles to tense (especially those in your neck and back, perhaps causing you a slight headache), plus you may feel nauseated—you know, like a million butterflies flapping their wings in your stomach! (*Familiar with that feeling? I'll bet that you are!*)

So when you feel these symptoms of "fight or flight" occur, remind yourself that it's only natural; it's only human!

Remember too that your body is merely reacting to what your *brain* tells it to do. So if you could control your brain . . . *but how?*

Well, while mind control is best left to the purveyors of infomercials, there are still a few things that you can do to ameliorate the effects of that damned little Fear Monster's doubt that's echoing in your head.

One thing is to do is what some actors and others in the public eye have done—create a *persona*. Let yourself become a character to play while you are giving your speech. If you allow yourself to become the character and don't stay "yourself" you can let that smooth talking rascal deliver your words! In other words: Play a part; Act a role.

Think about it: you're playing a role already, aren't you—Best Man; Father/Mother of the Bride/Groom; Maid/Matron of Honor, etc.? So there you go! _Become your role, let a little of your "self" go, and you'll feel a lot better delivering your speech_! Therefore, when you deliver your speech you can allow yourself to be slightly more objective and in character. Now you are _not_ Dad or the best friend— _you are your role_: the Father of the Bride, the Maid of Honor and so on! But, be careful:

Don't become so objective that you lose all emotion when delivering your speech and become more of a caricature than a character.

Of course, the more you actually practice saying your speech the easier it will be for you to deliver it. But you should also practice it using visualization. _Practice your speech in your mind!_ If you pretty much know your speech, picture yourself actually saying it. This technique is very effective, especially if you've been to where you will be speaking.

Lie down. Close your eyes, and picture yourself presenting your speech at the venue: emphasizing the words; making your gestures; picture yourself looking at the audience, scanning the crowd for familiar faces; raising your glass for the toast! Imagine yourself performing your speech with every little detail. The more often you do this in your mind, the easier it will be when you actually do it.

Actors do this all the time, and so do many athletes. How many times have you heard an athlete say that he/she just imagined (visualized) themselves making that basket, hitting that ball, making that goal, swinging that club, etc. and then they did it. Just as repeat performance in practice allows an athlete to build "muscle memory" so that their actions are almost automatic, visualizations "exercise" the brain and allow it to respond to the actual performance as an automatic, "no sweat" kind-a-thing. Hey, if actors and athletes effectively use this technique, you can use it too!

Some studies show that practicing visualization just before taking a quick fifteen to twenty-minute nap helps you remember the visualization more effectively.

(And, honestly, who couldn't use an excuse for an afternoon nap?)

Another trick, when you are speaking don't forget to look about the room for familiar faces and "play" to them. Focus on these people as your primary audience. And don't

forget to use them for affirmation as well. As I said before, I'm sure you have friends or family attending who will give you a confidence boost. After all, your family and friends are rooting for you!

You can also try some of Natures tricks. Do not drink alcohol or caffeine before speaking. Both can actually exacerbate the anxiety that you'll be feeling. You need something to help you calm down, not jack you up.

If you are going to drink something, some studies suggest that chamomile or bergamot teas can be relaxing.

So how about chemicals? No, not a tranquilizer (*NEVER* take one before a speech!) but something quite natural: like the scent of citrus or lavender! Peel an orange and sniff the citrus scent or take a whiff of lavender. Some research shows these scents can be uplifting and help relax you. An orange peel secreted in an old medicine bottle, or a small bottle of lavender scented perfume carried on your person and discreetly "sniffed" might just do the trick! For an even stronger scent, try sniffing orange or lavender *essential oils*. Try it when you practice. Hey, you lose nothing by trying!

What else? How about our old friend <u>PMA (Positive Mental Attitude)</u>! Repeat your mantra—"I *can* do this!", "I got this!" or whatever phrase you have chosen. Remember to close your eyes, inhale deeply through your nose, and exhale s-l-o-w-l-y through your mouth while mentally repeating your mantra over and over to yourself. Believe the words. Believe in yourself. Your repeated affirmation will be a very great and positive motivator!

· · ·

Now I know there is a lot more to fighting anxiety than that, but you'll read about some additional tips and tricks to battle that ol' fear monster in the next few chapters on delivering your speech.

For now, remember: proper practice procedure and *PRACTICE, PRACTICE, PRACTICE!* Think back to the speeches you have given in the past. Some were better than others were but I'll bet you learned from the mistakes you made in each and each succeeding speech became better. *(See, failure leads to success!)* When you look back on them now, I'll bet that you remember them without emotion . . . without fear. You gained insight into yourself and your performance with every speech you've ever given. And, with every speech, you gained a little more confidence.

From the vantage point of this experience, you understand that they were just a few passing moments in the timeline of your life, *just as this speech will be*.

And, let's be honest here, what is the worst that could happen? A few people think you are boring? *Who gives a red rat's a**!*

As I said before, your only real audience is The Couple who asked you to write and deliver a speech for <u>them</u> on this special occasion, and your well-written and beautifully delivered speech will do just that! Therefore, if you present a thoughtful, heart-warming, soulful speech that just happens to delight most of the assembled guests as well, then that's a plus!

Lastly, keep in mind that the more you practice your speech and the more you follow the tips provided in this book, the more *you will* come to believe both in the words you've written and in yourself!

<u>It's true: Be positive! Practice! The more you practice, the easier it gets; the more psyched *you* get, and the more confident you feel. And the more confident you feel, the more you'll lose yourself in the performance of your speech; and thus, you'll experience less fear!</u>

Believe in yourself, like your family and closest friends believe in you. YOU *CAN* DO THIS!

However, always remember that while the company of friends and family can certainly boost your self-confidence, the *best* company is always <u>your own</u>!

Practice, practice, practice—your speech; your delivery; the delivery tips (above and to follow) and prove to yourself what I already know:

You are one *helluva* person!

.   .   .

In summation, remember the speech William Shakespeare wrote for Hamlet when he addresses the performers he has hired to present the play before the king (Act III, scene 2):

"Speak the speech, I pray you, as I pronounced it to
   you, trippingly on the tongue: but if you mouth it,
   as many of your players do, I had as well the
   town-crier spoke my lines. Nor do not saw the air
   too much with your hand, thus, but use all gently;
   for in the very torrent, tempest, and, as I may say,
   the whirlwind of passion, you must acquire and beget
   a temperance that may give it smoothness."

My modern translation, dear speaker, is:

"Speak the speech you wrote, following your Speakers Symbols; practice it so it sounds natural and not forced; so that it sounds honest and from the heart; and unique: otherwise *anyone* could simply read what is written without your passion, drama or feeling. Follow your Speakers Symbols, knowing that you haven't used them willy-nilly, but through them, you have given life to your written words. Don't exaggerate your inflections or gestures. Just do as you've practiced and you'll give a splendid speech."

(Okay, I'm no Shakespeare! But you get the idea. Besides, some scholars debate whether Shakespeare was Shakespeare!)

And Finally . . .

Now that you have used the Speakers Symbols to capture your dramatic presentation, know *what* to practice and how *best to practice* your speech, you need only concern yourself with its timing.

(Don't have a stopwatch? Don't worry, chances are your mobile phone already has one as a function.)

Since The Couple has given you a suggested time limit for your speech, you should follow it as closely as possible. Time yourself while you practice to see if you need to slow down or speed up to fit your speech within the suggested time. Whichever it is, notate any changes with the Speakers Symbols!

As mentioned previously, most people deliver a speech at a rate of about 80 to 120 words a minute. They may speak faster in normal conversation, but delivering a speech requires a more leisurely rate of spoken words. So once you time yourself, you'll know your average rate and be better able to tailor your speech to fit your time limit.

By the way, don't worry about allowing time for laughter, applause, etc. that may occur during or after your speech. These are things to be hoped for and may or may not occur. So don't be tempted to plan pauses to wait for the thunderous roar of laughter you expect from a joke you put in your speech. IF it happens, great! Just don't make it a consideration when you practice the timing of your speech.

Once Again:

The one word that you may have noticed repeated over and over is: PRACTICE! After spending all that time writing your speech, it is important that you practice presenting it. Don't feel self-conscious about this. If you feel uncomfortable practicing: GET OVER IT! You'd practice a speech you were going to give in front of your boss, wouldn't you? Don't you think this is *at least* as important? Remember, *you* accepted this speaking engagement; and *this truly is an honor!* So, PRACTICE:

Don't muck it up!

Delivering YOUR Speech

Preparing to write a speech, actually writing a speech and preparing that speech for presentation are all preliminary events to the actual moment of delivering the speech. Delivering a speech takes work and preparation, especially lots of rehearsals. Practice may not make things perfect, but it can make things, well, perfect-er. (*Dammit, grammarians, leave me alone!*)

At the very least, preparation and practice lead to proficiency.

The following notes on delivery include recaps and expansions on what has already been covered, as well as a few additional tips. All are appropriate no matter what speech you give or where you give it.

+ Familiarity does *NOT* breed contempt! You have practiced your speech so you are familiar with it and your delivery will be the better for it. Now, are you familiar with *where* you will speak? If possible, visit your venue to see the general layout and become aware of its size, acoustics, etc. If you cannot get to the actual site of the reception, you might visit a similar reception hall, ballroom or auditorium so that you will have a visual reference.

+ <u>Knowing where you will speak will be a boost to your visualization</u>. It will allow you to lie down, close your eyes and visualize the delivery of your speech at that venue as you relax just before you fall asleep or just after you have awakened in the morning. (Some studies indicate that your mind is a little more relaxed and better able to process things at these times, so your visualization should have more of an impact on you if you practice it then.) The more you do this the more you will develop a sense of "been there, done that" and promote a positive mental attitude toward giving the speech.

+ Remember, this is the same advice given to athletes who relax and picture themselves making that jump, hitting that ball or sinking that putt. The more they visualize themselves jumping, swinging a bat, club or stick, or making that stroke, the more they have "practiced" it and the more confident they become that they can do it in reality—so you do the same!

+ And if you cannot get to the venue or a surrogate, just imagine a generic large room filled with seated guests. And look for familiar faces in the crowd.

+ Don't stress yourself out unduly! [*Except if you are a grammarian reading the last sentence!*] This speech is only a few minutes of a much longer event, and it's only a very few minutes of your life. Also, be aware that, as in Life, there are always things that may happen that are beyond your control—you start to get a cold and your voice sounds "funny," the microphone doesn't work, or your speech is unexpectedly moved forward in order, and so on. Things *could* go wrong—but probably won't. And even if they do: Don't sweat what you *can't* control. Remember, the one thing that you can definitely control is YOURSELF!

+ Accept the fact that public speaking *is* stressful and that, no matter how prepared you feel you are, *YOU WILL FEEL A LITTLE STRESSED!* So let it happen. Accept it. Just DON'T PANIC! I've already explained what's happening to your body when you experience extreme anxiety, and you know how to cope with it. One way is to remember: PMA! (*As they used to say in cheesy horror thrillers, "It's ALL IN YOUR MIND!"*) Stay calm and know this: despite the exceptional presentation of your literary musings, most people won't even remember what you said an hour after you finish your speech—let alone remember any nervousness you might have shown!

+ But what they *will* remember is *how* you spoke and how you made them *feel*. You have practiced this. You've notated your speech with Speakers Symbols and you know just how to effectively deliver your words. You *will* manipulate the emotions of your audience; you know you *will* have your listeners in the palm of your hands and that *there won't be a dry eye in the house!*

You've got the power! <u>Be confident!</u>

+ <u>Remember too that the people you will be speaking to are *your* audience.</u> They will be sympathetic to you and damned glad it's not them up there having to make a speech! And don't forget, for the few minutes that you are speaking, they are there to see *you*: You are the focus of their attention! (*Hey, no pressure, right?*) But remember: the audience is on your side! Like you, they were invited to share this event and want it to be as enjoyable as possible. Everyone is there for a common purpose, so view your audience as friends that you haven't quite met yet—but friends none-the-less! They wish you all their best because they hope that your well-written and well-delivered speech *will* be enjoyable. In other words, they have high hopes and low expectations. And since *you* know that both your speech and presentation is killer, you *know* that your speech and presentation *will blow them away!*

+ <u>As you speak, include your "new friends" in the speech by making eye contact with them.</u> Select a few tables (front, left and center) to glance to on occasion. And perhaps you have family members or friends in the audience that you can make eye contact with. By doing this you are not excluding any part of the audience from your glance. This way everyone will feel included even if your gaze does not fall directly upon them.

+ You should also occasionally look at the person(s) you are addressing in your speech, even if the audience knows to whom you are speaking. As to The Couple, you need only make eye contact with them when making your toast—the one part of your speech you *have* memorized, *right*?

+ So remember, the audience is *NOT* your enemy! Besides, although you are addressing everyone in the room, your only *real* audience is The Couple who asked you to speak.

+ It is very important to remember to smile and breathe! Hopefully, you have notated stops for breath in your notes! It is remarkable how often amateur speakers seem to gasp for breath or appear to be winded during a speech.

+ Your speech may include some amusing remarks. If you have included a humorous anecdote or joke, remember to pause and wait for an audience reaction. I hope that the reaction will be laughter. However, if your joke is "underappreciated" (or worse, *it bombs*!) say something like, "You may not get it now; but later, when you are driving home, you'll get it and then you'll *laugh* and *laugh* . . ." And then don't worry about it. Just proceed with your speech. After all, <u>you are there to be entertaining, not to be *THE* entertainment!</u>

+ If you find yourself becoming a little choked up, finding a slight tremble in your voice or feeling your eyes well up with tears, *it's okay!* You don't have to fight it; you can <u>let these positive emotions get to you!</u> All it does is make you more human.

  In fact, not only are emotions permitted on this occasion but also are probably welcomed! Just pause for a moment, clear your throat or take out your hankie and dab your eyes. The audience will understand; and more than that, they will sympathize with you. I said that when you were done speaking there wouldn't be a dry eye in the house—and that included your eyes too!

+ Finally, when you are done, pause for just a few seconds, sit down slowly or walk over and calmly take your seat to the appreciative applause of everyone there—and congratulate yourself on an outstanding performance!

. . .

On The Day of the Rehearsal or Reception

Note: Although the content of your speech will differ depending on whether you are delivering a rehearsal speech (looser, less formal, more emotional, more personal) or a reception speech (tighter, more formal, slightly less emotional, personal, and more general), the delivery of each is very much the same. Also, these general tips are valid for *any* speech you may give in the future. So this book is of benefit far beyond your wedding rehearsal/reception speech. How 'bout that!

Here you are, at the rehearsal or reception. This is it! Prep, practice, and rehearsal have led you to this moment. You are taking your seat at the dais, or wherever, ready for the event to start. As you do so, remember the following tips and suggestions to help you make your speech more successful.

Do you find yourself a little anxious? Perhaps your palms are a little moist and a bead or two of sweat now shows on your forehead? Not to worry—remember, it's only natural. *RELAX!*

Remember: Keep a Positive Mental Attitude! You've got this! Your speech is as perfectly written (and will soon be as perfectly delivered) as you could make it. Heck, there won't be a dry eye in the house!

Remember too, that you've practiced, and practiced, and practiced delivering the speech. Your notes are notated

. . . every subtle gesture, every emotive emphasis, is carefully marked — *YOU ARE READY!*

(*Come on, admit it: in reality, you've got confidence up the wazoo!*)

. . .

Just in case, though, here is a recap of some of the notes we have covered:

+   Maintain positivity!

+   Accept the butterflies! You're expected to be a little nervous!

+   Talk to the person(s) (family or friends) there with you. Use them both for comfort and to psyche you up.

+   No one else around you? Self-affirmation! Repeat your mantra: "I *KNOW* I got this!"

+   Remember to smile and laugh — both are "good medicine" for anxiety.

+   In fact, now would be a great time for a joke. Listen for one in the conversation of your fellow speakers, remember a favorite one of your own, or make a careful observation of the venue and audience: There is always something or someone at a wedding you can joke about, to yourself if to no one else. (Hey, I know it's snarky and cruel, but I have yet to be at a wedding where *something or someone* wasn't just "a little off." Maybe it's someone's crazy Uncle—and most families have one—who showed up in a tux *and flip-flops!*)

+ Do something physical to loosen up. Shake your arms a little. Roll your shoulders (this really helps with the muscle tension in your neck). Sit up extra straight, then slouch a little and repeat a couple more times. When sitting at the dais or table, you can always wiggle your toes in your shoes, tap your feet, shake your legs—just don't be *too* obvious should you do it. Repeat each "exercise" as necessary.

+ Close your eyes for a few seconds, smile to yourself and picture a quiet place where you might normally relax.

+ Raise both hands to your head and press your fingers just a little above the bony ridge of your eyebrows and press and rub slightly for a few seconds. I'm told that it sends a little extra blood to the spot and tends to make you a little less tense.

+ Take a deep breath by inhaling through your nostrils, holding it for a few seconds, and exhaling s-l-o-w-l-y through your mouth. You may have to do this a few times, but you should feel yourself relax a little.

+ Try and wear a citrusy smelling cologne or perfume, or bring a small bottle to sniff. Bring an orange peel in an old medicine bottle if you have to! Some studies have shown that the scent of citrus is calming and may reduce the stress hormone (cortisol) that's in your blood. Others say that a strong scent of lavender will also work. Heck, why not bring 'em both!

+ Now, try that deep breathing again using your citrus or lavender scents. That should do the trick!

+ Review your index cards/papers. Seeing and holding them will give you additional confidence.

+ Sip some water just before your speech or use a quick dissolve mint or candy to combat a dry mouth. If you have been served an alcoholic beverage for toasting throughout the speeches, try *not* to touch it! No Dutch courage! (*I heard the sirens of the PC police even as I wrote that!*) Ask for a glass of water, if one hasn't already been provided, and use the wine or champagne just for the toasts.

+ If a restroom is nearby and you can get to it, splash some cool water on your face to freshen up. If there isn't one close by or you can't get to it, keep some facial wipes with you to "freshen up" before you speak. (Be careful with your makeup, ladies!) At worse, you can always use a clean hankie to pat your forehead and face. (NEVER use your napkin!)

+ And while you listen to the other speakers before you, note their phrasing and watch their delivery. I'll bet you'll notice a flaw or two. Don't find joy in their accidental mishaps, but do feel a little more confident in your own abilities. After all, *you'll* do GREAT! You will be better than most of the other speakers (and that is no mindless mantra because chances are it will be true!) and if any of the others have read this book and—like you are doing—and are following its guidelines, then you will be *at least* as good as they are! And that ain't too shabby!

+ When you do get up to speak, you will either stand up from your seat and speak or walk over to a microphone. Whichever it is, do so calmly. Stand up s-l-o-w-l-y. (Don't jump up from your seat or rush to the mic.)

+ Look at both The Couple and your audience. Smile confidently. As you do so, take a deep breath.

+ Stay calm! Chances are your audience won't even notice your nervousness, but if *you* are a little self-conscious of it, you can always make a joke about it. Perhaps you could say something like: "You think

I'm nervous? Hey, I just have to *say* it; but you poor people have to *watch* me do it!"

(Remember, they *are* on your side. "There, but for the grace of God . . ." and all that.)

+ And, lastly, once again remind yourself:

"I've have practiced this! Everyone speaking will just as nervous! The audience is on my side! I wrote one *helluva* speech! I'm psyched! In fact, I'm itching to get up and deliver it! I *KNOW* I *CAN* DO THIS!"

Okay, you've just been introduced . . . it's your turn! Smile . . . take a deep breath . . . slowly stand up and . . .

Go get 'em!

AT LAST!

Okay; you're finally here!

This is *YOUR* special section detailing everything about the speech you will actually give for the role you play — Father of the Bride, Best Man, and so on.

Here you'll find the specific details you'll need to write, practice and deliver the Wedding Speech that's right for you.

You have already learned a lot from the previous chapters, now you need to apply that knowledge to your specific role.

Read carefully, understand what you need to do to dutifully fulfill your role, and thank you for reading up to this point. Continue to take your notes because soon you will have all the information you need to actually begin putting pen to paper or fingers to keyboard.

So Just When Will You Speak?

The Couple, or their wedding planner, should have already informed you of the order of speakers so you will know when you will be called upon. They should also have informed you whether you will be announced by an MC or by the previous speaker and if you will have to announce the person speaking after you.

While the usual order of speakers is given here, remember: It's The Couple's special day and they may choose any order they want, and they may change it at the last minute!

Should they do this, you needn't worry because you have a well-written, well-rehearsed speech that you can confidently deliver at any time. PMA, right?

The Traditional Order of Speakers at . . .

. . . the REHEARSAL

The Host (Father/Patents of the Groom or whoever paid for the event, or the MC)

The Best Man

The Maid/Matron of Honor (the Chief Bridesmaid)

Groomsmen and Bridesmaids

The Mother's and Father's of the Bride and Groom who will <u>not</u> speak at the Reception

Anyone else who would like to speak ("open mic")

The Couple (who close the speeches with a toast)

. . . the RECEPTION

English Traditional

Father of the Bride

Groom

Best Man

Traditional

Best Man

Groom

(Miscellaneous Others)

Father of the Bride

Modern Traditional

Father of the Bride

Best Man

M/MoH (Maid/Matron of Honor)

Groom

Other Arrangements

Best Man

M/MoH

Father of Bride

The Couple

. . . .

Best man

Groom

Bride

Father of the Bride

. . . .

The MC

Best Man

M/MoH

The Couple

Parents of The Couple

Same-Sex

Best Man

Maid/Matron of Honor

Second partner's Father and/or Mother

First partner's Father and /or Mother

Second partner [if not as a couple]

First partner [or as a couple]

Note: Remember, these charts are merely for general information. The Couple will choose the order of speakers and may wish to include nontraditional speakers, such as favorite relatives or honored guests. It is also possible, in fact, more than likely, that at the reception The Couple may wish to speak *after* the last speaker to "officially" close the reception before the party begins!

. . .

Note: For all the speeches that follow, you can often substitute "partner" for "Bride" or "Groom" or switch out "son" or "daughter" as needed.

The Father of the Bride Speech
(Father of the Second Partner)

This speech is usually the first one given at a traditional English wedding reception. In this traditional order of speakers, it is first because he (presumably) paid for the wedding and so acts as both host and "featured" speaker, and offers the *first* toast to The Couple. However, today that may or may not be the case. In other traditions, the Father of the Bride speaks last and offers the *final* toast to the newlyweds. They might even ask you to speak first and then again to conclude all of the speeches with a final toast.

If you are the Father of the Bride, The Couple should have informed you of the order of speakers, so you may have to adjust some of the following depending on when you speak.

Yours is usually the most cherished speech of the event because you are saying goodbye to your "little girl" and (reluctantly) welcoming a new man into her life. Your speech is expected to be slightly more formal, yet more personal and touching, considering a father's relationship with his daughter.

Note: You may need to re-read the chapter on "Special Considerations."

The general duties of your Father of the Bride speech include:

+ Thanking everyone for attending and sharing in this special moment

+ If appropriate, a quick "thank you" to the Maid/Matron of Honor for helping your daughter

+ Welcoming the Groom and his parents into the family

+ Telling a few stories about your daughter – tender, sentimental, heartfelt memories are actually preferred

+ A story or statement about her charm, beauty, and grace

+ Offering a father's view of how your daughter has changed since meeting the Groom and how hard it is to let her go to start a family of her own

+ Giving your sincere best wishes for The Couple

+ Offering a toast to the newlyweds

Father of the Bride Speech Template

<u>INTRODUCTION</u>

Who you are (if you are not introduced)

Welcoming and thanking the attendees

A special welcome to the Groom's parents

Who are you speaking about? (Primarily about the Bride)

Some short anecdote(s) (sincere, humorous)

Short Quotation

[See and "Quotes" in Appendices]

BODY

A longer anecdote(s) (sincere, humorous)

A Quote

[See both "Sample Speech Bodies" and "Quotes" in Appendices]

CLOSING

Focus on seriousness; how much you'll miss your "little girl"

Sincere Best Wishes for The Couple

TOAST

(Serious or humorous, but *always* sincere)

[See sample "Toasts" in Appendices]

An Example of a Father of the Bride Speech

"I have the pleasure of being (<u>Bride's name</u>) father and it is both an honor and a delight to welcome you here today/tonight and to thank you all for coming.

"I am especially happy to welcome (<u>Groom's name</u>) and his wonderful parents (<u>Groom's parent's names</u>) here today/tonight . . . and into the family.

"It has been a real pleasure watching my little (<u>Bride's name</u>) grow up and turn into the fine woman she is. This is both a sad and joyous occasion for me, as I say "goodbye" to my little girl and "hello" to the beautiful wife she has become.

"It's so true what they wrote that, 'A son is a son until he takes him a wife; but a daughter's a daughter for all a Dad's life;' so if will indulge a father, I'd like to tell you something about (<u>Bride's name</u>) . . . (Tells a story or two about his daughter's childhood, some tender moment, etc.)

"She has always been beautiful to me; I have watched a gracious girl turn into a wonderful woman. And though it is hard to let her go, I know (<u>Groom's name</u>) sees her as I do, and loves her too, well, *almost* as much!

"I couldn't believe that at first—and no father can—but (<u>Groom's name</u>) has proven himself to me, and I want him to know that I trust him with my dearest little girl. In fact, I am proud of him; indeed, the both of them! And I wish them . . . (A sincere wish for The Couple; perhaps something from "Sample Speech Bodies" in the Appendices.)

"Please join me and raise your glass in a toast . . . (the toast you've chosen.)"

[Remember to supplement your speech with quotes and materials from the Appendices.]

.   .   .

The Best Man Speech

Note: As for all speeches given, adjust the information presented here to conform to the particular circumstances of the event. You may need to re-read the section on "Special Occasions."

If you are the Best Man, your speech can be first, last or somewhere in the middle. Once The Couple informs you when you will be speaking, you can adjust some of the following depending on when you speak.

The Best Man is usually the most anticipated speech of the event because you are expected to be the "funny one" and your speech the most entertaining. Your speech can be a little less formal and more personal, considering your friendship with the Groom, and the broad nature of your speech.

The general duties of the Best Man speech include:

+ Thanking the Groom for his toast to the Maid of Honor and Bridesmaids (*if* the Groom's speech has already been given)

+ Telling how you met the Groom and stories about your friendship

+ Telling some humorous (often a little risqué, but NEVER embarrassing) jokes or anecdotes about the Groom

+ Offering an insider's view of how The Couple met; how the Bride has changed the Groom for the better, and other positive general comments on The Couple

+ The reading of emails, cards, letters, etc. from those unable to attend (You should be given an edited list of these by The Couple)

+ Thanking your "counterpart," the Maid/Matron of Honor and the Bridesmaids

+ Thanking the Groomsmen for their assistance to you

+ Thanking the Groom for choosing you as Best Man

+ Offering a toast to the Bride

Best Man Speech Template

INTRODUCTION

Who you are (if you are not introduced)

Thanking the Groom for his toast to the Bridesmaids (if he has done so already)

Some short anecdote(s) (sincere, humorous) about how you met the Groom and your friendship with him

Short Quotation

[See both "Sample Speech Bodies" and "Quotes" in Appendices]

BODY

A longer anecdote(s) (sincere, humorous, usually slightly bawdy) about the Groom

An insider's look at how meeting the Bride changed him

[See both "Sample Speech Bodies" and "Quotes" in Appendices]

CLOSING

Focus on seriousness

Read the congratulatory cards, telegrams, emails, etc. from those unable to attend the wedding that were given you by The Couple

"Thank You" to the Maid/Matron of Honor and the Bridesmaids, *if* the Groom hasn't already done this

A very sincere "Thank You" to the Groom for choosing you as the Best Man. Tell him that you'll miss him as your best friend, but now he's got someone even more special in his life.

TOAST

Best Wishes for The Couple

(Serious or humorous, but *always* sincere)

[See sample "Toasts" in Appendices]

An Example of a Best Man Speech

"Good day/evening, I'm _____, and I have the honor to be (<u>Groom's name</u>) best man. Which begs the question, (<u>Bride's name</u>), if *I* am the BEST man, why did you marry (<u>Groom's name</u>)?

"Oh, well . . .

"Seriously, I want to thank you, (Groom's name), for your kind words and toast to (Maid of Honor's name) and our lovely Bridesmaids. You are as gracious as I am handsome!

"I can kid (Groom's name) because I have known him . . . (a story about how you met and became friends; followed by another one that shows his basic character — always good naturedly! It might be appropriate to use a quote here to reiterate the point of your story).

"I remember the time . . . (this is where you'd tell a slightly risqué anecdote or two about the Groom. The purpose is to tease him in a good-natured "roast" and not to embarrass him.)

"But I was amazed at how much he has changed since he met (Bride's name). She has really changed him for the better . . . and I, for one, thank her for it! (Here's where you tell a brief anecdote or two about your observations as to how she has changed your friend and how much he is in love with his partner.)

"I am so happy to share this special occasion with you, but some of your family and friends couldn't be here. Many sent their congratulations and I'd like to share a few of them with you. (Here you read the list of "congrats" given you by The Couple. They should have notated these to indicate who sent them, "____'s Uncle John says . . .")

"To which I can only add my own sincere thanks, (Groom's name), for choosing me to fill this honorable position and for allowing me to remain your best friend;

well up to now! Now you have a truer friend and confidant than I could ever hope to be. And I thank you (Bride's name) for allowing me to become your friend as well. It is truly an honor. I wish you both . . . (your sincere best wishes or "Speech Body", followed by your toast.)

[Remember: you can supplement your speech with quotes and materials from the Appendices]

. . .

Speeches for Everyone Else: Non-traditional Speakers

Note: As for all speeches given, adjust the information presented here to conform to the particular circumstances of the event. You may need to re-read the sections "Special Occasions" and "A Special Note for Stepparents."

Okay, you have been asked to give a speech, but you played no role at the wedding. You have no "official duties" to perform with your speech, so what do *you* say?

The following are the "usual" non-traditional speakers and their order. (However, The Couple may change the order as they wish: it's their wedding!):

~ The Maid/Matron of Honor (Chief Bridesmaid)

~ Mother of the Bride

~ Father/Parent(s) of the Groom

~ Bridesmaids and Groomsmen

~ The Honored Guest*

~ Other Family Members**

Read the brief sections here for your particular speech and, if you choose, go back and re-read the chapters dealing with the general information on preparing to write, writing, practicing and delivering a speech so you are well prepared.

Remember: Just because *you* don't consider yourself a "featured" speaker, The Couple chose you to speak and think of you as important to the success of the event.

Use the following as a guide, and supplement it with information from the Appendices, if you choose.

* This speaker is usually someone very special to The Couple, such as mentor, a boss, a neighbor who watched the Bride or Groom grow up, etc. This speaker follows the

Rehearsal template, as this speech is always more personal and less formal. (See chapter, "The Rehearsal Speech")

** If you are a brother, sister, Uncle or another family member who has been asked to speak, you might also want to use a speech similar to that given at the wedding rehearsal. (See chapter, "The Rehearsal Speech") Your speech is expected to be more emotional and heartfelt considering your family relationship.

. . .

The Maid/Matron of Honor Speech

(Chief Bridesmaid)

Note: This non-traditional speaker is becoming more and more traditional. As for all speeches given, adjust the information presented here to conform to the particular circumstances of the event. You may need to re-read the section on "Special Considerations."

If the Maid/Matron of Honor is to speak, her speech is usually scheduled *after* the Best Man's speech. The reason for this is that her duties to the Bride are similar to that of the Best Man's to the Groom. Therefore, her speech should also be similar to the Best Man's speech.

In other words, if you are the Maid/Matron of Honor, your speech should be an entertaining speech and a "funny one" at that. Like the Best Man's speech, hers can be a little less formal and more personal, considering her friendship with the Bride and the general nature of the speech.

The general duties of the Maid/Matron of Honor include

+ Offering sincere thanks to the Bride for honoring you with the position of Chief Bridesmaid

+ Thanking the Groom for his toast to the Bridesmaids (*if* the Groom's speech has already been given)

+ Offering your personal thanks to the Bridesmaids for their help; (and, if applicable, thanking them for assisting you in organizing this event)

+ Complimenting the Best Man and Groomsmen

+ Telling everyone how you met the Bride and about your friendship

+ Telling some humorous (often a little risqué, but NEVER embarrassing) jokes or anecdotes about the Bride

+ Offering an insider's view of how The Couple met and how the Groom has changed your friend for the better, and other positive general comments on The Couple

+   Offering a toast to the Groom

[Supplement the speech with information in the Appendices]

As the Chief Bridesmaid, you have had a lot to do with the wedding and reception, and the Bride should recognize your efforts in her speech, when and *if* it is given. The Bride will certainly acknowledge your work personally if she hasn't thanked you publicly. It is most likely though that the Groom will mention and thank you in *his* speech if the Bride is not going to speak. It is also possible that the Father of the Bride will acknowledge you because the Maid/Matron of Honor is usually someone the Bride's family has known for some time and certainly appreciates all that you have done for his daughter during the wedding preparations. And certainly, the Best Man will mention you as his "counterpart."

An Example of a Maid/Matron of Honor Speech

"It is an honor to be here today/tonight and a very great honor to be chosen as Maid/Matron of Honor! It was a privilege to be Chief Bridesmaid to such a wonderful court of ladies, and I thank them all. They are each as beautiful as the Groomsmen are handsome! Speaking of which, thank you (<u>Best Man's name</u>) for your kind words.

"I first met (<u>Bride's name</u>) (story of first meeting) . . . and we've been friends ever since! She is a wonderful person, but I recall one time . . . (humorous/slightly risqué anecdote). But so much has changed since she met (<u>Groom's name</u>). (Tell an inside story of how the Bride has changed since meeting her Groom).

"I sincerely wish you both the best. I know (<u>Bride's name</u>) that we will never be as close again; and that you may have found a 'new best friend' in (<u>Groom's name</u>) but if I am a little jealous, it is only because I know that he is so great for you! I will certainly miss our time together, but I wish you both love, and I know that now you two are together, neither of you will ever miss love for it will always be there in each other's touch and kiss!

(Perhaps insert a speech body from the Appendices)

Conclude with your toast: "To (<u>The Couple's names</u>)!"

[Supplement the speech with information in the Appendices]

. . .

The Mother of the Bride's Speech
(The Second Partner's Mother's Speech)

Note: Remember, if the Mother of the Bride is speaking *in the role of* the <u>Father</u> of the Bride, then her speech would fill *those* duties. See "The Father of the Bride's Speech" and alter as appropriate. It is also possible that she will be asked to simply rise and give a short, sincere toast.)

There is no usual spot for this speech so The Couple may place it anywhere.

As the Mother of the Bride, you have a different perspective than the father. You have been instrumental in guiding your daughter from childhood to womanhood — and all the celebrations and trials that go with that. Because of this unique view of the Bride, your speech can (and should) be very sentimental.

The general duties of the Mother of the Bride speech include:

+ Thanking everyone for attending and sharing in this special moment

+ Acknowledging the parents of the Groom, welcoming them into the family and thanking them for raising a fine son

+ Telling a few stories about your daughter (the more tender, sentimental and heartfelt the better)

+ Offering a mother's view of how your daughter has changed since meeting the Groom

+ Offering a mother's perspective—and advice—on marriage and starting a family

+ Concluding with your sincere best wishes for The Couple and . . .

+ A toast to the newlyweds

An Example of a Mother of the Bride Speech

"It is a great pleasure to see you all here today/tonight for this glorious celebration of my daughter and her wonderful husband! And I especially want to thank (<u>name of Groom's parents</u>) for raising such a splendid young man and for the pleasure of joining our two families together to share in the joys yet to come.

"It is so hard for me to imagine that my little girl is married! I remember . . . (sentimental story/stories about the Bride). She has grown and changed so much, especially since she met (<u>Groom's name</u>). (Story of *how* she has changed).

"I can offer a few words of advice to you, my darling daughter . . . (Perhaps advice from the "Sample Speech Bodies" in the Appendices)

"And someday if you are blessed with as wonderful a child as you were to me you'll finally understand how I feel. (Perhaps insert a sentimental recollection.) However, a family is in the future. For now, I offer you my love and sincere best wishes for a long and happy life together.

(Your toast. Perhaps something like: "To my darling daughter and her handsome husband!"

[Supplement the speech with information in the Appendices]

. . .

The Father/Parent(s) of the Groom

(Father/Parents of the First Partner)

If the Groom's father/parents are to speak it would be sometime *after* the Father of the Bride. (Unless the Father of the Bride speech is the "closing" speech.) One or both parents may speak, as determined by The Couple.

The speech should include these general topics:

+ A thank you to the Father of the Bride for his remarks and—if appropriate—hosting (paying for) the event

+ Complimenting both parents of the Bride for having raised a wonderful person and trusting his son to care for her now

+ Offering compliments to the Bride and welcoming her into the family as his new "daughter"

+ Congratulating his son on marrying such a wonderful person

+ Offering some "fatherly" advice (sincere and/or humorous) on marriage

+ Thanking everyone for attending

+ Offering a toast to The Couple

Note: The Groom's mother may rise and stand beside her spouse as he speaks or she may speak separately. If she is to speak, the Groom's Mother's speech would follow the same general guidelines as above, and she can also use the Mother of the Bride speech for a reference.

An Example of a Father of the Grooms Speech

"It is an honor to be here today/tonight and I especially want to recognize and thank (<u>Father of the Bride's name</u>) for his kind remarks and (if appropriate) for hosting this wonderful reception! And also, my sincere thanks to him and his lovely wife (<u>Mother of the Bride's name</u>) for raising such a wonderful daughter and for trusting my son with her care. I am pleased that our two families are together to enjoy the future with our two terrific kids!

"And what a splendid and lovely woman you are (<u>Bride's name</u>)! My son may have taken a wife but I have gained a delightful new daughter! I am so happy to have you in the family!

"I am truly happy that my son has shown great common sense in allowing (<u>Bride's name</u>) into his heart and into his life. You made a wonderful choice of someone with whom to share the rest of your life. You know that you weren't always so smart. I remember . . . (humorous anecdote about son).

"But here you are an 'old married man'. Since I am one too, let me give you some fatherly advice . . . (sincere, sentimental and/or humorous comment(s) on marriage, perhaps something from the "Sample Speech Bodies" in the Appendices)

"I am so very grateful that all of you could be here to join in this celebration to my son and 'my new daughter' ('his new partner') and I wish them . . . (the toast)."

[Supplement the speech with information in the Appendices]

. . .

Bridesmaids and Groomsmen Speeches

One representative on each group's behalf usually gives these speeches because a full court of Groomsmen and Bridesmaids would take about half an hour or more to get through. These speeches are very *non*traditional at a reception. Most commonly, these speeches are given at the rehearsal; but that is not to say that The Couple hasn't scheduled a spot for them at the reception. If you are to speak, you should have already been informed as to which event and when you will speak at that event.

As to the speech itself, don't worry—this is usually the briefest and easiest speech of all. If you are speaking as a representative of either group (or *both* groups) you would offer a general speech. If a few of you are to speak, then your speeches can be more personal.

In general, this speech/these speeches should contain:

+ Thanks to the Bride/Groom (as appropriate) for the honor of being a Bridesmaid/Groomsman

+ Perhaps a personal story or Speech Body/Quote

+ Sincere best wishes to her/him on their marriage

+ A toast to The Couple

An example might be:

"I (we) want to thank (<u>name of Bride and/or Groom</u>) for allowing me (us) the honor of serving as a Bridesmaid/Groomsman (Bridesmaids/Groomsmen) and sharing in an *extra*-special aspect of this very special day.

"I remember . . . (anecdote or Speech Body/Quote)

"I (we) wish them luck, happiness and, especially, love as they begin their lives together."

(Close with a toast. Perhaps something as simple as "To (Bride and Groom's name), May you always share the joy I (we) have found with you today and may it always honor you both as I (we) feel honored to have been a part of this glorious day/night!"

The Guest

Or

"I was just sitting there and suddenly this guy with a video camera shows up . . ."

<u>Warning</u>: Wedding receptions can often
be unpredictable:

Expect the Unexpected!

You're a guest at the reception. The speakers have spoken, dancing has started, champagne and drinks flow—a good time is being had by all! You're relaxed, smiling, having a conversation with those at your table when unbeknownst to you, the MC suddenly walks over a shoves a microphone in your face and expects you to say "a little something" and make a toast to the happy couple!

Whoa!

Or worse, it's the videographer who will capture your words (and awkwardness) *<u>forever</u>*!

Your mind races, and suddenly goes blank! You smile, but you feel your face flush and your palms become moist. *What do you say? What do you do?*

Well, you're reading this book, so if the above scenario was to happen (and it very well could!) <u>you'd know just what to do!</u> First, you'd know that you *do NOT panic!*

You rise, if appropriate, and speak directly into the microphone or camera and say:

"I am honored to be here to share in this wonderful moment with these two very special people. May the love you both share this day live always in your hearts. To ___ and ___!" (Of course, if in your momentary panic you forget The Couple's names, you can just say, "To the happy couple!")

Or words to that effect.

The key is to go into the reception with the expectation of having to say *something*; either to The Couple themselves, perhaps in the reception line, or as presented in the scenario above.

If all else fails or you simply don't want to memorize a lengthy toast, then you can always say one of these quick toasts:

"___ and ___, I wish you all the love in the world, always!"

"My best wishes for a long, happy life together!"

"Thank you for allowing me to share this beautiful occasion! I wish you both the beauty of this (day/night) throughout your lives together!"

"No two people deserve happiness as much as you both do! Happiness always!"

"God Bless you both today/tonight and always! Congratulations!"

"May the joy you find (today/tonight) be yours forever!"

There! Six simple toasts. Try and memorize at least two —just in case some others at the reception have read this book also . . . and "steal" *your* toast!

In Conclusion

Time To Get Started

If you have read this book straight through until now, I believe that you will have an easier time writing your speech. If you began writing it before now, I hope that you will go back, refer to your notes (*you did take notes, didn't you?*) and adjust your speech as needed to make it even better.

I also hope that you will have discovered that writing a wedding speech isn't as daunting a task as you first thought and that as you read about it, you found the process comparatively easy—at least, compared to your initial fears.

Speech writing of any kind is a difficult process, be it for school or business—and especially for weddings. So when you finish writing and practicing your speech, congratulate yourself and feel proud!

Once you finally deliver it, I hope that you sit back, relax, and enjoy the rest of the rehearsal and/or reception knowing that your speech delighted all and was greatly appreciated by The Couple. (And, if The Couple asked for a copy of your speech for their Memory Box, know that your words will be appreciated again every anniversary when they read your speech!)

I also hope that the next time you have to write and deliver a speech, for whatever event or occasion, you will remember to re-read this book and use the tips and tricks presented here. Such things as the three-part outline, Speakers Symbols and the practice and delivery tips will be very useful. This book has value beyond just writing your Wedding Speech.

Thank You again for allowing me to be, in some small way, a part of your very special day.

Good Luck and I wish you all the best!

J. Thomas Steele

P.S.

If you haven't taken notes thus far, I leave several of the next pages and a few more at the end of the book for your use. Remember, your notes will help you with future speeches for other celebrations, school, or work.

APPENDICES

Please note:

I remind you that the information in these appendices is only *some* of the information you might find if you researched on your own. They are not meant to be a complete source for your use. My sole intent was to provide you with as much basic research as possible to save you time and effort.

(In other words, just because a quote you like ain't here doesn't mean that you can't use it!)

The Origins of Wedding Words

No doubt you will hear these words at the rehearsal, the wedding ceremony, and the reception, so why not show off your knowledge of their origins. You might just impress your fellow guests or, at worst, out bore the bores you might run into!

The English word "matrimony" is derived from the Latin word *matrimonium*. That word has at its root the Latin word *mater* or "mother". This implies the main reason for the marriage—to have legitimate children who could, therefore, continue the line and receive an inheritance from the mother and father.

"Marriage" is Middle English, from the Old French *marier* which itself derives from the Latin word *maritare*, but all mean "to wed."

"Wedding" comes from the Old English word "wed" which means "a solemn promise." The act of giving that promise, the "wed-ing", was symbolized by the ring given to the Bride which showed that the husband would honor his pledge.

"Vow" comes from the Latin. It means "vote," to make a solemn statement.

"Bridal" may have originated from the term "Bride's ale," which she and her Groom drank after the wedding.

"Wedlock" comes from the Old English, meaning the marriage vow in action and thus the state of marriage. It does *not* mean that you are locked in a marriage!

Cheat Sheets

Preparing YOUR Wedding Speech

+ Understand the honor being given you: YOU were chosen by The Couple to speak at what is probably the most important day of their lives!

+ Allow yourself time to prepare and write your speech; do NOT try to "wing it"!

+ Know the role you play and understand its traditional duties

+ Think about your relationship with one or both members of The Couple

+ Note any special memories that might be appropriate for your speech

+ Consider researching and including additional anecdotes and quotes

+ Consider what to say as a sincere toast to The Couple to end your speech

+ Understand there will be a time limit for your speech, so stay within that time

And for Heaven's sake use these Appendices for quotations and speech samples! I worked hard to pull together these appropriate quotes and write these speech bodies for your use or reference. Take advantage of the Appendices and save yourself some time and research.

The Traditional Order of Reception Speakers

English Traditional

Father of the Bride

Groom

Best Man

Traditional

Best Man

Groom

(Miscellaneous Others)

Father of the Bride

Modern Traditional

Father of the Bride

Best Man

M/MoH (Maid/Matron of Honor)

Groom

Other Arrangements

Best Man

M/MoH

Father of Bride

The Couple

. . . .

Best man

Groom

Bride

Father of the Bride

. . . .

The MC

Best Man

M/MoH

The Couple

Parents of The Couple

Same-Sex

Best Man

Maid/Matron of Honor

Second partner's Father and/or Mother

First partner's Father and /or Mother

Second partner [if not as a couple]

First partner [or as a couple]

General Wedding Speech Template

INTRODUCTION

Who you are (if not introduced)

Who are you speaking about? (the Bride; the Groom; both?)

Some short anecdote(s) (sincere, humorous)

A short Quotation [if appropriate]

BODY

A longer anecdote(s) (sincere, humorous)

A longer Quote [if appropriate]

CLOSING

Focus on seriousness

"Thank You's" (as appropriate if not given before)

Sincere Best Wishes for The Couple—
if not included in the Body

TOAST

(Serious or humorous, but *always* sincere)

USE THESE APPENDICES TO SUPPLEMENT WITH SPEECH BODIES, QUOTES, AND QUOTES

Writing YOUR Wedding Speech:

General Notes

+ The ideal speech should be about 5 minutes long; about 800 words. The Couple will give you this information.

+ If not introduced, introduce yourself to the audience. Always explain your relationship to The Couple.

+ Always make any story you tell "universal"— easily relatable by the audience.

+ Always make your stories positive—NEVER embarrass The Couple!

+ A cute story is more appreciated than a flat joke.

+ To highlight your own story—or if you cannot find the words to express yourself—use quotes, poems, song lyrics, etc.

+ Always keep your writing honest and sincere.

+ When complementing The Couple, use a few appropriate adjectives: but don't gush!

+ If you are a member of the Wedding Party, remember to "Thank" as appropriate to your role.

Speaker's Symbols

The more common Speaker's Symbols — and the ones you will most likely use — are:

Pronunciation: If you do not know how to pronounce a word and look it up in a dictionary, you will see these marks. They help you understand whether the sound is a short or long sound, show accents and syllables, and stress or emphasis. If you do decide to use an unfamiliar word in your speech, copy the dictionary pronunciation! You do not want to mispronounce the word when you deliver your speech!

Ex: Pronunciation (pr*uh*-nuhn-see-**ey**-sh*uh*)

Inflection: this indicates the rise or drop in the pitch of your voice when you pronounce the word. It is usually written as a slightly curved arrow and placed above the word. The arrow points **up** for a rise in pitch and **down** for a drop in pitch.

Ex: "What did you do?"

Emphasis: To emphasize the word(s) or phrase, underline it once for emphasis or twice for a particularly hard emphasis. If typing, you can use italics for single emphasis or underlined italics for double (hard) emphasis.

Ex: "<u>What</u> did you do?" "*What* did you <u>*do*</u>?"

Intonation: Like inflection, it means to add additional emotion or feeling to the word(s) or phrase by use of the tone of your voice. This symbol is usually a wavy line beside or under that part of your speech.

Ex: "I wish you both ≈Love!"

Pause or Stop: You probably use these symbols every time you write! The common symbol for pause is the comma (",") and the period (".") for a stop! You can also use a single diagonal line ("/") for a common pause or a double diagonal ("//") for a longer pause. Use an ellipsis ("...") for an emphasized (longer) pause. For a full stop, there is nothing better than the good, old period - PERIOD!

Ex: "I'm not sure what will happen, but // I'm ready for it."

"I'm not sure what will happen ... but I'm ready for it."

Pause to Take a Breath: Please remember to breathe when you speak! That would seem obvious, but some speakers tend to take a deep breath before they begin and then forget to breathe as they speak! To be sure you remind yourself to pause for a breath, use the bracket symbols with a capital B between them ("[B]").

Mannerisms: If your speech requires you to gesture for a particular emphasis or to make a point, you can use the parentheses with a capital G—for Gesture— between them ("(G)"). Of course, you have to remember *what* gesture you have to make!

Notes on Delivering Your Speech

You *WILL* be nervous! Stay calm and *Don't Worry* about it; worrying about it only makes it worse!

Gain confidence by:

+ Outlining the key phrases of your speech on an index card(s)/paper(s)—(The only thing you should completely memorize is your toast to The Couple)

+ Keeping everything in perspective—it's really not a "do or die" kind of thing;

+ Spending substantial time practicing your speech; it's not "do or die", but it *is* important!

+ Practicing speaking in front of a mirror to see your body language;

+ Practicing in front another person and encouraging their feedback, having them record you on their cell phone so you can see your performance;

+ And if you can, go the actual site of the rehearsal/reception so that it becomes familiar to you.

On The Day of the Rehearsal or Reception

+ Remember to accept the butterflies! You're expected to be a little nervous!

+ Talk to the person(s) (family or friends) there with you. Use them for comfort and to psyche you up.

+ Remember to both smile and laugh—they are "good medicine" for anxiety;

+ Perhaps smell some citrus or lavender scent.

+ Do something physical to loosen up. Perhaps just shake your arms a little.

+ Take a few deep breaths—in through your mouth and slowly out through your nose.

+ Look at your index cards/papers. Seeing them will give you some confidence.

+ Sip some water just before you speak or use a quick dissolve mint or candy to combat a dry mouth.

+ If you think you'll need them, keep some facial wipes with you to "freshen up" before you speak. (Be careful with your makeup, ladies!)

How to Properly Use a Microphone

+ Most likely the M.C. or host will have already turned the microphone on and preset the volume during a sound check prior to the event.

+ If holding the microphone, grip it firmly—but not too tightly—in the middle of its handle. Judge the firmness of your grip by the weight of the microphone—some are heavier than others. And *please* be careful not to touch or move any buttons on the handle—you might turn the mic off!

+ Most microphones (handheld or stand) should be held about 4 to 6 inches from your mouth, but *never* more than a hands-width away.

+ Keep the microphone held at a 45-degree angle to your mouth.

+ Speak into the <u>top surface</u> of the mic. If you hold the mic, DO NOT hold it to the side or close to your chest, as this can cause distortion.

+ If you hear the dreaded sound of feedback, hold the mic *closer* to you and speak. Holding it farther away from you will probably let it pick up other noises and make the feedback worse! (Feedback most often comes from the mic being too close to a speaker. Usually, the venue will not have speakers near where you will be speaking, but if they do, you may have to step away from them to resolve the issue.)

+ When you do speak, enunciate, pronounce, and speak confidently—after all, you have rehearsed your speech and it should sound great! You will probably be holding your written speech in one hand and the microphone in the other, and your hands may shake slightly (that's okay!). You have marked your pauses, emphasis', etcetera— so just present the speech as you rehearsed it.

+ And how do you rehearse holding the micro- phone? Hold a hairbrush and practice—just like you did when you were 10 years old and swore you were on your way to becoming a rock star!

Bible Readings

These are but a few of the "usual" readings used for many weddings. However, you may have many favorites of your own that you choose to use.

The references that I have chosen are from three varied translations of the Bible. The Douai-Rheims, the first translation of the Latin Vulgate in English (and the first English translation to be officially authorized by the Roman Catholic Church); the Protestant translation of the Bible, the King James Bible (the Church of England's translation authorized by King James I); and it's revised version, the American Standard Version (1901).

The verses presented here are:

<u>Old Testament</u>: Genesis 1: 26-31, Genesis 2: 21-25, Song of Solomon 8: 6-7, Proverbs 3: 1-6; 13-16;

<u>New Testament</u>: 1 Corinthians 13, Ephesians 3: 16-21, Colossians3: 12-17, John 4: 7-21

Douai-Rheims

Genesis 1

²⁶ And he said: Let us make man to our image and likeness: and let him have dominion over the fishes of the sea, and the fowls of the air, and the beasts, and the whole earth, and every creeping creature that moveth upon the earth. ²⁷ And God created man to his own image: to the image of God he created him: male and female he created them. ²⁸ And God blessed them, saying: Increase and multiply, and fill the earth, and subdue it, and rule over the fishes of the sea, and the fowls of the air, and all living creatures that move upon the earth. ²⁹ And God said: Behold I have given you every herb bearing seed upon the earth, and all trees that have in themselves seed of their own kind, to be your meat: ³⁰ And to all beasts of the earth, and to every fowl of the air, and to all that move upon the earth, and wherein there is life, that they may have to feed upon. And it was so done. ³¹ And God saw all the things that he had made, and they were very good. And the evening and morning were the sixth day.

Genesis 2

²¹ Then the Lord God cast a deep sleep upon Adam: and when he was fast asleep, he took one of his ribs, and filled up flesh for it. ²² And the Lord God built the rib which he took from Adam into a woman: and brought her to Adam. ²³ And Adam said: This now is bone of my bones, and flesh of my flesh; she shall be called woman, because she was taken out of man. ²⁴ Wherefore a man

shall leave father and mother, and shall cleave to his wife: and they shall be two in one flesh. ²⁵ And they were both naked: to wit, Adam and his wife: and were not ashamed.

Song of Solomon 8

⁶ Put me as a seal upon thy heart, as a seal upon thy arm, for love is strong as death, jealousy as hard as hell, the lamps thereof are fire and flames. ⁷ Many waters cannot quench charity, neither can the floods drown it: if a man should give all the substance of his house for love, he shall despise it as nothing.

Proverbs 3

¹ My son, forget not my law, and let thy heart keep my commandments. ² For they shall add to thee length of days, and years of life, and peace. ³ Let not mercy and truth leave thee, put them about thy neck, and write them in the tables of thy heart. ⁴ And thou shalt find grace, and good understanding before God and men. ⁵ Have confidence in the Lord with all thy heart, and lean not upon thy own prudence. ⁶ In all thy ways think on him, and he will direct thy steps.

¹³ Blessed is the man that findeth wisdom, and is rich in prudence: ¹⁴ The purchasing thereof is better than the merchandise of silver, and her fruit than the chief and purest gold: ¹⁵ She is more precious than all riches: and all the things that are desired, are not to be compared to her. ¹⁶ Length of days is in her right hand, and in her left-hand riches and glory. ¹⁷ Her ways are beautiful ways, and all her paths are peaceable.

1 Corinthians 13

¹ If I speak with the tongues of men and of angels, and have not charity, I am become as sounding brass, or a tinkling cymbal. ² And if I should have prophecy and should know all mysteries and all knowledge, and if I should have all faith, so that I could remove mountains, and have not charity, I am nothing. ³ And if I should distribute all my goods to feed the poor, and if I should deliver my body to be burned, and have not charity, it profiteth me nothing. ⁴ Charity is patient, is kind: charity envieth not, dealeth not perversely, is not puffed up, ⁵ Is not ambitious, seeketh not her own, is not provoked to anger, thinketh no evil: ⁶ Rejoiceth not in iniquity, but rejoiceth with the truth: ⁷ Beareth all things, believeth all things, hopeth all things, endureth all things. ⁸ Charity never falleth away: whether prophecies shall be made void or tongues shall cease or knowledge shall be destroyed. ⁹ For we know in part: and we prophesy in part. ¹⁰ But when that which is perfect is come, that which is in part shall be done away. ¹¹ When I was a child, I spoke as a child, I understood as a child, I thought as a child. But, when I became a man, I put away the things of a child. ¹² We see now through a glass in a dark manner: but then face to face. Now I know in part: but then I shall know even as I am known. ¹³ And now there remain faith, hope, and charity, these three: but the greatest of these is charity.

Ephesians 3

¹⁶ That he would grant you, according to the riches of his glory, to be strengthened by his Spirit with might unto the inward man: ¹⁷ That Christ may dwell by faith in your hearts: that, being rooted and founded in charity, ¹⁸ You

may be able to comprehend, with all the saints, what is the breadth and length and height and depth, [19] To know also the charity of Christ, which surpasseth all knowledge: that you may be filled unto all the fulness of God. [20] Now to him who is able to do all things more abundantly than we desire or understand, according to the power that worketh in us: [21] To him be glory in the church and in Christ Jesus, unto all generations, world without end. Amen.

Colossians 3

[12] Put ye on therefore, as the elect of God, holy and beloved, the bowels of mercy, benignity, humility, modesty, patience: [13] Bearing with one another and forgiving one another, if any have a complaint against another. Even as the Lord hath forgiven you, so do you also. [14] But above all these things have charity, which is the bond of perfection. [15] And let the peace of Christ rejoice in your hearts, wherein also you are called in one body: and be ye thankful. [16] Let the word of Christ dwell in you abundantly: in all wisdom, teaching and admonishing one another in psalms, hymns, and spiritual canticles, singing in grace in your hearts to God. [17] All whatsoever you do in word or in work, do all in the name of the Lord Jesus Christ, giving thanks to God and the Father by him.

1 John 4

[7] Dearly beloved, let us love one another: for charity is of God. And every one that loveth is born of God and knoweth God. [8] He that loveth not knoweth not God: for God is charity. [9] By this hath the charity of God appeared towards us, because God hath sent his only begotten Son into the world, that we may live by him. [10] In this is charity:

not as though we had loved God, but because he hath first loved us, and sent his Son to be a propitiation for our sins. [11] My dearest, if God hath so loved us, we also ought to love one another. [12] No man hath seen God at any time. If we love one another, God abideth in us: and his charity is perfected in us. [13] In this, we know that we abide in him, and he in us: because he hath given us of his spirit. [14] And we have seen and do testify that the Father hath sent his Son to be the Saviour of the world. [15] Whosoever shall confess that Jesus is the Son of God, God abideth in him, and he in God. [16] And we have known and have believed the charity which God hath to us. God is charity: and he that abideth in charity abideth in God, and God in him. [17] In this is the charity of God perfected with us, that we may have confidence in the day of judgment: because as he is, we also are in this world. [18] Fear is not in charity: but perfect charity casteth out fear, because fear hath sin. And he that feareth is not perfected in charity. [19] Let us, therefore, love God: because God first hath loved us. [20] If any man say: I love God, and hateth his brother; he is a liar. For he that loveth not his brother whom he seeth, how can he love God whom he seeth not? [21] And this commandment we have from God, that he who loveth God love also his brother.

King James Bible

Genesis 1

[26] And God said, Let us make man in our image, after our likeness: and let them have dominion over the fish of the sea, and over the fowl of the air, and over the cattle, and over all the earth, and over every creeping thing that creepeth upon the earth. [27] So God created man in his *own* image, in the image of God created he him; male and female created he them. [28] And God blessed them, and God said unto them, Be fruitful, and multiply, and replenish the earth, and subdue it: and have dominion over the fish of the sea, and over the fowl of the air, and over every living thing that moveth upon the earth. [29] And God said, Behold, I have given you every herb bearing seed, which *is* upon the face of all the earth, and every tree, in the which *is* the fruit of a tree yielding seed; to you it shall be for meat. [30] And to every beast of the earth, and to every fowl of the air, and to every thing that creepeth upon the earth, wherein *there is* life, *I have given* every green herb for meat: and it was so. [31] And God saw every thing that he had made, and, behold, *it was* very good. And the evening and the morning were the sixth day.

Genesis 2

[21] And the LORD God caused a deep sleep to fall upon Adam, and he slept: and he took one of his ribs, and closed up the flesh instead thereof; [22] And the rib, which the

LORD God had taken from man, made he a woman, and brought her unto the man. ²³ And Adam said, This *is* now bone of my bones, and flesh of my flesh: she shall be called Woman, because she was taken out of Man. ²⁴ Therefore shall a man leave his father and his mother, and shall cleave unto his wife: and they shall be one flesh. ²⁵ And they were both naked, the man and his wife, and were not ashamed.

Song of Solomon

⁶ Set me as a seal upon thine heart, as a seal upon thine arm: for love *is* strong as death; jealousy *is* cruel as the grave: the coals thereof *are* coals of fire, *which hath a* most vehement flame. ⁷ Many waters cannot quench love, neither can the floods drown it: if *a* man would give all the substance of his house for love, it would utterly be contemned.

Proverbs 3: 1-6

¹ My son, forget not my law; but let thine heart keep my commandments:² For length of days, and long life, and peace, shall they add to thee. ³ Let not mercy and truth forsake thee: bind them about thy neck; write them upon the table of thine heart: ⁴ So shalt thou find favour and good understanding in the sight of God and man. ⁵ Trust in the LORD with all thine heart; and lean not unto thine own understanding. ⁶ In all thy ways acknowledge him, and he shall direct thy paths. ¹³ Happy *is* the man *that* findeth wisdom, and the man *that* getteth understanding. ¹⁴ For the merchandise of it *is* better than the merchandise of silver, and the gain thereof than fine gold. ¹⁵ She *is* more precious than rubies: and all the things thou canst desire are not to

be compared unto her. [16] Length of days *is* in her right hand; *and* in her left-hand riches and honour. [17] Her ways *are* ways of pleasantness, and all her paths *are* peace. [18] She *is* a tree of life to them that lay hold upon her: and happy *is every one* that retaineth her.

1 Corinthians 13

[1] Though I speak with the tongues of men and of angels, and have not charity, I am become *as* sounding brass, or a tinkling cymbal. [2] And though I have *the gift of* prophecy, and understand all mysteries, and all knowledge; and though I have all faith, so that I could remove mountains, and have not charity, I am nothing. [3] And though I bestow all my goods to feed *the poor*, and though I give my body to be burned, and have not charity, it profiteth me nothing. [4] Charity suffereth long, *and* is kind; charity envieth not; charity vaunteth not itself, is not puffed up, [5] Doth not behave itself unseemly, seeketh not her own, is not easily provoked, thinketh no evil; [6] Rejoiceth not in iniquity, but rejoiceth in the truth; [7] Beareth all things, believeth all things, hopeth all things, endureth all things. [8] Charity never faileth: but whether *there be* prophecies, they shall fail; whether *there be* tongues, they shall cease; whether *there be* knowledge, it shall vanish away. [9] For we know in part, and we prophesy in part. [10] But when that which is perfect is come, then that which is in part shall be done away. [11] When I was a child, I spake as a child, I understood as a child, I thought as a child: but when I became a man, I put away childish things. [12] For now we see through a glass, darkly; but then face to face: now I know in part; but then shall I know even as also I am

known. ¹³ And now abideth faith, hope, charity, these three; but the greatest of these *is* charity.

Ephesians 3

¹⁶ That he would grant you, according to the riches of his glory, to be strengthened with might by his Spirit in the inner man; ¹⁷ That Christ may dwell in your hearts by faith; that ye, being rooted and grounded in love, ¹⁸ May be able to comprehend with all saints what *is* the breadth, and length, and depth, and height; ¹⁹ And to know the love of Christ, which passeth knowledge, that ye might be filled with all the fullness of God. ²⁰ Now unto him that is able to do exceeding abundantly above all that we ask or think, according to the power that worketh in us, ²¹ Unto him *be* glory in the church by Christ Jesus throughout all ages, world without end. Amen.

Colossians 3

¹² Put on therefore, as the elect of God, holy and beloved, bowels of mercies, kindness, humbleness of mind, meekness, longsuffering; ¹³ Forbearing one another, and forgiving one another, if any man have a quarrel against any: even as Christ forgave you, so also *do* ye. ¹⁴ And above all these things *put on* charity, which is the bond of perfectness. ¹⁵ And let the peace of God rule in your hearts, to the which also ye are called in one body; and be ye thankful. ¹⁶ Let the word of Christ dwell in you richly in all wisdom; teaching and admonishing one another in psalms and hymns and spiritual songs, singing with grace in your hearts to the Lord. ¹⁷ And whatsoever ye do in word or deed, *do* all in the name of the Lord Jesus, giving thanks to God and the Father by Him.

1 John 4

⁷ Beloved, let us love one another: for love is of God; and every one that loveth is born of God, and knoweth God. ⁸ He that loveth not knoweth not God; for God is love. ⁹ In this was manifested the love of God toward us, because that God sent his only begotten Son into the world, that we might live through him. ¹⁰ Herein is love, not that we loved God, but that he loved us, and sent his Son *to be* the propitiation for our sins. ¹¹ Beloved, if God so loved us, we ought also to love one another. ¹² No man hath seen God at any time. If we love one another, God dwelleth in us, and his love is perfected in us. ¹³ Hereby know we that we dwell in him, and he in us, because he hath given us of his Spirit. ¹⁴ And we have seen and do testify that the Father sent the Son *to be* the Saviour of the world. ¹⁵ Whosoever shall confess that Jesus is the Son of God, God dwelleth in him, and he in God. ¹⁶ And we have known and believed the love that God hath to us. God is love; and he that dwelleth in love dwelleth in God, and God in him.¹⁷ Herein is our love made perfect, that we may have boldness in the day of judgment: because as he is, so are we in this world. ¹⁸ There is no fear in love; but perfect love casteth out fear: because fear hath torment. He that feareth is not made perfect in love. ¹⁹ We love him, because he first loved us. ²⁰ If a man say, I love God, and hateth his brother, he is a liar: for he that loveth not his brother whom he hath seen, how can he love God whom he hath not seen? ²¹ And this commandment have we from him, That he who loveth God love his brother also.

American Standard Version

Genesis 1

26 And God said, Let us make man in our image, after our likeness: and let them have dominion over the fish of the sea, and over the birds of the heavens, and over the cattle, and over all the earth, and over every creeping thing that creepeth upon the earth. 27 And God created man in his own image, in the image of God created he him; male and female created he them. 28 And God blessed them: and God said unto them, Be fruitful, and multiply, and replenish the earth, and subdue it; and have dominion over the fish of the sea, and over the birds of the heavens, and over every living thing that moveth upon the earth. 29 And God said, Behold, I have given you every herb yielding seed, which is upon the face of all the earth, and every tree, in which is the fruit of a tree yielding seed; to you it shall be for food: 30 and to every beast of the earth, and to every bird of the heavens, and to everything that creepeth upon the earth, wherein there is life, [I have given] every green herb for food: and it was so. 31 And God saw everything that he had made, and, behold, it was very good. And there was evening and there was morning, the sixth day.

Genesis 2

21 And Jehovah God caused a deep sleep to fall upon the man, and he slept; and he took one of his ribs, and closed up the flesh instead thereof: 22 and the rib, which Jehovah God had taken from the man, made he a woman,

and brought her unto the man. 23 And the man said, This is now bone of my bones, and flesh of my flesh: she shall be called Woman, because she was taken out of Man. 24 Therefore shall a man leave his father and his mother, and shall cleave unto his wife: and they shall be one flesh. 25 And they were both naked, the man and his wife, and were not ashamed.

Song of Solomon 8

6 Set me as a seal upon thy heart, As a seal upon thine arm: For love is strong as death; Jealousy is cruel as Sheol; The flashes thereof are flashes of fire, A very flame of Jehovah. 7 Many waters cannot quench love, Neither can floods drown it: If a man would give all the substance of his house for love, He would utterly be contemned.

Proverbs 3—1-6

1 My son, forget not my law; But let thy heart keep my commandments: 2 For length of days, and years of life, And peace, will they add to thee. 3 Let not kindness and truth forsake thee: Bind them about thy neck; Write them upon the tablet of thy heart: 4 So shalt thou find favor and good understanding In the sight of God and man. 5 Trust in Jehovah with all thy heart, And lean not upon thine own understanding: 6 In all thy ways acknowledge him, And he will direct thy paths.

13 Happy is the man that findeth wisdom, And the man that getteth understanding. 14 For the gaining of it is better than the gaining of silver, And the profit thereof than fine gold. 15 She is more precious than rubies: And none of the things thou canst desire are to be compared unto her. 16

Length of days is in her right hand; In her left hand are riches and honor.

1 Corinthians

[1] If I speak with the tongues of men and of angels, but have not love, I am become sounding brass, or a clanging cymbal. [2] And if I have [the gift of] prophecy, and know all mysteries and all knowledge; and if I have all faith, so as to remove mountains, but have not love, I am nothing. [3] And if I bestow all my goods to feed [the poor], and if I give my body to be burned, but have not love, it profiteth me nothing. [4] Love suffereth long, [and] is kind; love envieth not; love vaunteth not itself, is not puffed up, [5] doth not behave itself unseemly, seeketh not its own, is not provoked, taketh not account of evil; [6] rejoiceth not in unrighteousness, but rejoiceth with the truth; [7] beareth all things,

believeth all things, hopeth all things, endureth all things. [8] Love never faileth: but whether [there be] prophecies, they shall be done away; whether [there be] tongues, they shall cease; whether [there be] knowledge, it shall be done away. [9] For we know in part, and we prophesy in part; [10] but when that which is perfect is come, that which is in part shall be done away. [11] When I was a child, I spake as a child, I felt as a child, I thought as a child: now that I am become a man, I have put away childish things. [12] For now we see in a mirror, darkly; but then face to face: now I know in part; but then shall I know fully even as also I was fully known. [13] But now abideth faith, hope, love, these three; and the greatest of these is love.

Ephesians 3

[16] that he would grant you, according to the riches of his glory, that ye may be strengthened with power through his Spirit in the inward man; [17] that Christ may dwell in your hearts through faith; to the end that ye, being rooted and grounded in love, [18] may be strong to apprehend with all the saints what is the breadth and length and height and depth, [19] and to know the love of Christ which passeth knowledge, that ye may be filled unto all the fullness of God. [20] Now unto him that is able to do exceeding abundantly above all that we ask or think, according to the power that worketh in us, [21] unto him [be] the glory in the church and in Christ Jesus unto all generations forever and ever. Amen.

Colossians 3

[12] Put on therefore, as God's elect, holy and beloved, a heart of compassion, kindness, lowliness, meekness, longsuffering; [13] forbearing one another, and forgiving each other, if any man have a complaint against any; even as the Lord forgave you, so also do ye: [14] and above all these things [put on] love, which is the bond of perfectness. [15] And let the peace of Christ rule in your hearts, to the which also ye were called in one body; and be ye thankful. [16] Let the word of Christ dwell in you richly; in all wisdom teaching and admonishing one another with psalms [and] hymns [and] spiritual songs, singing with grace in your hearts unto God. [17] And whatsoever ye do, in word or in deed, [do] all in the name of the Lord Jesus, giving thanks to God the Father through him.

1 John 4

⁷ Beloved, let us love one another: for love is of God; and every one that loveth is begotten of God, and knoweth God. ⁸ He that loveth not knoweth not God; for God is love. ⁹ Herein was the love of God manifested in us, that God hath sent his only begotten Son into the world that we might live through him. ¹⁰ Herein is love, not that we loved God, but that he loved us, and sent his Son [to be] the propitiation for our sins. ¹¹ Beloved, if God so loved us, we also ought to love one another. ¹² No man hath beheld God at any time: if we love one another, God abideth in us, and his love is perfected in us: ¹³ hereby we know that we abide in him and he in us, because he hath given us of his Spirit. ¹⁴ And we have beheld and bear witness that the Father hath sent the Son [to be] the Saviour of the world. ¹⁵ Whosoever shall confess that Jesus is the Son of God, God abideth in him, and he in God. ¹⁶ And we know and have believed the love which God hath in us. God is love; and he that abideth in love abideth in God, and God abideth in him. ¹⁷ Herein is love made perfect with us, that we may have boldness in the day of judgment; because as he is, even so are we in this world. ¹⁸ There is no fear in love: but perfect love casteth out fear, because fear hath punishment; and he that feareth is not made perfect in love. ¹⁹ We love, because he first loved us. ²⁰ If a man say, I love God, and hateth his brother, he is a liar: for he that loveth not his brother whom he hath seen, cannot love God whom he hath not seen. ²¹ And this commandment have we from him, that he who loveth God love his brother also.

. . .

Short readings or quotes from The Couples favorite portion of their religious text or book of worship are usually always welcome.

One *caveat*, though: If the text is not from your own religious tradition, it still deserves your respect and so does the beliefs of The Couple. Whenever using such a text, always read from it with sincerity and *gravitas*, and treat the text with respect.

You may, of course, choose to use quotations from your own preferred religious texts, but always ask The Couple first if they would allow it.

Sample Speech Bodies

These speech bodies range from insightful to humorous; and with a tweak here and there, are appropriate for almost any speaker.

<<<<<<<>>>>>>

"As you go through your lives together, you start off *loving* each other because you *need* each other. But over time, as you grow together, you'll find you *need* each other because you *love* each other."

"There is no true life without Love. It is Love that transcends all understanding. There is no reason to it and no explanation for it. It, simply, *is*! Love is what creates life from mere existence. Love is what animates you through each day and propels you through each night. It excites, it baffles, it is a pleasure and it is a pain. There may be as many tears as there are smiles in Love. It may be soul-crushing and yet, lifts your spirit to the heavens! There is no way to capture it; it exists nowhere and everywhere. If you look for it, it may evade you. When you stand still and don't even think about it, then it may appear! It is joy and sorrow, day and night, high and low: confusing and contradictory. It is everlasting, but brief—for Love must be measured in a lifetime. So cherish both it and your beloved. Today your simple individual strivings, your mere *existence* ended. You have each found Love, so today you truly begin to *live*, for there is no true life without Love!"

. . .

"Cherish each other; cherish your Love. Realize that, like life itself, it is fleeting. You found each other and you have each found Love with one another. But take heed, for anything that can be found can be lost. Do not dwell on that possibility, but always keep it in mind; for it makes your time together all the sweeter. Enjoy your togetherness, and recognize the preciousness of every moment. Understand how fragile a thing is Love. Practice forgiveness and understanding; keep your eyes, ears, and heart always open to each other. Find joy in each other and

171

your togetherness. There is no greater gift than the love you share; appreciate it, and each other. Cherish each other. Cherish your love."

. . .

"There are no certainties in life. So as you begin your lives together, stare deeply into each other's eyes for a moment, find your still point and then turn and look toward the future. Whatever waits, awaits you both. Yes, the future is the unknown; but don't worry, for the future is merely that second that came before this one. Each second flows from the future to the present, and into the past. It is nothing more.

"My sincerest wish is that you enjoy each and every precious second you are together. And as you travel from each and every uncertain second to the next, know that the future holds Love—and Love has no age and no boundaries. Find the joy in all it presents to you. Find hope in all it gives. Find the promise in all that awaits you. And find yourselves there, in the future, always and together; and always and together in Love."

. . .

"The laws of <u>physics</u> tell us that there is no such thing as a perpetual motion machine. It simply cannot exist. You cannot have something that forever gives without taking, and never gives out: for everything has a limit. But the laws of <u>life</u> tell us that there *is* a limitless, inexhaustible source of power; that the more you take from it, the more

172

there is—and the more you give, the more you get in return.

"It is a source available to all though many never truly find it. It is something to be sought, but yet may be found by *not* looking! It is often the rational outcome of irrational events. It has the power to make you collapse under its weight or lift you up to the heavens. It can make the strongest weak and the weakest strong. It can make a beggar of kings and a king of beggars. It can make the mighty weep with either sadness or joy. It lifts the scales of the past from your eyes and lets you behold a world and future transformed.

"Yet, if you hold out your hand to grab it, to take hold, you find it cannot be held; it can only be felt. And if it ever is to be contained, it is not to be held in mere hands where it may slip through the fingers; nor can it be kept in the mind where it would rattle among the trivial. No, if it is to be contained at all, it must reside in the heart.

"It exists forever. It takes a moment and stretches it into eternity, and creates an eternity in a mere moment. It possesses you completely, yet in that possession, you find a freedom you have never known. It has no age and knows no death. It is what I wish you now and always . . . it is Love!"

· · ·

"I can say this much about you both: neither of you is a very good artist. I've seen your doodles and I can tell you, *I'd* never put them on *my* refrigerator door! So let me take a

173

moment and teach you, if not about how to draw, a little about color—in particular, the colors of Love.

"Love is not a single color, nor does it come in only one shade. It has many hues and depths. It is composed of subtleties from the palette of heaven itself, which gives it life and meaning.

"It can be red from anger; black from misunderstanding; green from envy, blue from sadness and purple from the bruises life often gives you. Yet you will find each color's edges blended so you don't know where any *one* color begins or truly ends. It can be a boring beige or a shimmering metallic; rusty brown or shiny silver. It is these contrasting colors that make life—and Love—a work of art.

"But mostly it is painted in yellow, like the warm sun that shines upon us; and blues—not the sad hue—but the color of a late autumn sky at noon, cloudless and clear. It is orange, like the fruit of summer; and gray, like the clouds that bring the blessed rain that revitalizes both the brown earth and us. It is a myriad of russets, muted yellows, fiery reds, and fading greens, like the leaves of autumn. And whatever colors appear on the canvas of your life from now on, you will find that they are *always* tinged with gold.

"My wish is that you find your canvas to be both as broad as a landscape, and as intimate as a miniature portrait. May your future together be painted in every color from heaven's crayon box; subtle as a watercolor, bold as an abstract; with lots of space for you both to 'paint-by-numbers' and add your own splashes of color. Your life together now provides you with all the colors on your palette. You will find that now as you go through your lives together, you have both become artists, and now may choose the colors of your Love."

. . .

"Marriage is a very curious thing. It is not just comprised of two people, but two people *in Love*; and it is love that makes all the difference. No one has ever really explained how it is that two people become one, yet remain two. They stay themselves, yet Love allows them to twist together, like the individual thin strands that transform a brittle string to a strong rope.

"And no one has explained how it is that they can never seem to get enough love from each other, nor seem to give each other enough. The more one takes, the more the other gives; absorbing it merely to give it back in return. Nor can it be explained how it is that they can look at each other, not as in a mirror that reflects only their singular image, but a reflection that lets each be perfectly themselves, with every blemish, every mark visible and yet still be beloved.

"But you both have journeyed to this point and now embark on your destiny: to find the even deeper mysteries of Love. And it is an adventure that no *one* can go on, for it can only be searched for *together;* because what is sought is found both without yourself and yet within each other. Marriage is that never-ending search; an exploration both blissful and blistering. It is a treasure hunt to find life's pot of gold.

175

"As you begin your journey of discovery, my wish is that that it be a long one. And that the roads you travel along your route always be smooth; but if there are bumps and pot-holes that shake you, remember, you have each other to cling to.

"May your adventures together take you far and wide, and may you always travel *happily* together. And, that at the end of your adventure, you discover that the treasure you both have each sought lies no farther away than the reach of each other's embrace."

. . .

"Eden was a paradise. Marriage, is, well . . . less so! But it is still a great place to be! Just remember to share the chores as you tend the garden of your togetherness. Till the ground well and prepare the soil for the seeds of Love you'll sow. Pull out any weeds of discord that grow. Tread lightly and avoid the thorns that must surely exist in any garden.

"Let your garden be fragrant with the sweet scent of Love's flowering and let it perfume you both. Breathe deeply and let it pervade your souls.

"In that tranquil spot, I pray the sun always shines warmly upon you, that the rains are gentle and cool; that you find the Love you have planted grows into an orchard of strong trees; each bearing sweet blossoms, and from them even sweeter fruit.

"I pray your marriage is a garden of delights, forever tended, together, in Love."

. . .

"Time holds still for no one; even those in Love. The key is to find grace in aging together and always seeing the beauty in each other. In the years ahead as your eyes fail, *see with your heart*; as your hearing goes, *listen with your heart*. As your touch becomes less sensitive, and nothing smells or tastes as sweet as it once did—*take it to heart*. And when your heart itself finally fails, know that all that is in it, all that Love, lives on."

. . .

"To be perfectly honest, (<u>*Grooms name*</u>), I wasn't sure of 'the boyfriend' hanging around my house and sneaking into my daughter's life . . . and slowly stealing the heart of my little girl. I wasn't sure I'd like you. (*pause*) But I do! I am proud of you and I'll hold you to your promise to always Love and care for her.

"Like the man said: "My son is my son till he has got him a wife, but my daughter's my daughter all the days of her life."

And I am especially proud of (<u>*Daughter's name*</u>), **my** little girl, for choosing to wed a man who is *almost* as smart, strong and good-looking as her Dad!"

. . .

"Marriage, some say, is like opening a can of worms. However, in reality, it is more like opening a can of alphabet soup! Every spoonful of life together spells something different! It can be very confusing, so to make it easier for you, I've alphabetized some of the things you'll deal with in your lives together.

"Accomplishment, Advice—both asked for and unwanted; Age; Anger; Anniversaries (don't dare forget today's date!); Attitude—both good and bad; Beauty; Beer (if you're lucky!); Belief in each other; Birthdays (again, don't forget the date—but don't remember her age, my boy!); Children [if appropriate]; Confidence; Courage; Decisions; Dreams (tread lightly on each other's!); Education (and trust me, you'll learn something new about each other every day!); Experience; Failures; Family; Fear; Freedom; Fun; Glory; God; Grief (of which I wish you as little as possible); Happiness (of which I wish you loads); Hatred; Heart (and its' unbelievable capacity for love); Honesty; Hope; Imagination; In-Laws (and you are both *very* lucky to have the ones you do, because sometimes in-laws are more like out-laws!); Inspiration; Insults; Jealousies; Justice; Kindness; Love; Luck; Magic; Money (and how quickly it disappears); Opportunities (both lost and found); Pain; Problems; Romance; Sadness; Sex [pause a second, then clear your throat]; Sorrows; Tears; Time (and like money, how quickly it too disappears); Trust; Understanding; Weakness; Wisdom; Work; Worry; and, finally, Zoo—because that is what married life can seem to be sometimes!

"But of all of these words and the many, many meanings that you will both attach to them over your years together, none is more important than Love. Those four letters drive every other word on my list; because every word there has some component of Love in it. For Love is indeed in all the things that you'll share together.

"So let me conclude by offering my sincerest wish that you live a long, happy life together . . . and that you savor your alphabet soup!"

. . .

"At this particular moment in time, the two of you have created something unique, yet it is shared by all who have chanced upon it. You have transformed each other's reality, and indeed the worlds', by joining together. And what, exactly, is it that you two have done? You have brought into existence the compelling power of Love.

"And what is Love? No one can define it. No one can understand it. Yet it is the ultimate truth; the essential reality. It lies at the heart of what you have created today.

"May it always guide you, inspire you and comfort you; as indeed you must do with each other. May you understand that Love is a living thing and not a mere sentiment; that it needs to be nourished by your togetherness and understanding even as it nourishes you. May it always be the brightest thing you see sparkle in each other's eyes and hear whispered in each other's every word. And may you both always share the uniqueness of *your* Love."

179

. . .

"Marriage is just the beginning. As you both keep and grow together, your marriage will progress. But please understand that progression implies work, and marriage certainly demands work.

"It may require some heavy lifting, even some down and dirty labor. It can be tedious toil and for what some may see as very low pay—but then again, who can put a price on a kiss? Marriage isn't easy; it requires focus, attention, and commitment; each of which is a never-ending task.

"But it is a pleasant task; indeed, the best job there is! What's more, you don't have to do it by yourself—you have each other. And it is this working *together* that will make your marriage a success. Remember, keep your hopes high and your expectations low and you'll always be pleased with your progress!

"So, here's to the work ahead; to those burdens and joys; to that toil and trouble. Best of all, here's to all those kisses!"

. . .

"It isn't often that a (father/mother/parent) can say that was a pleasure raising a (son/daughter). (*pause*) And I wish *I* could!

"But (name) was a typical kid: a little devil when awake and an angel only when (he/she) was sound asleep! All of you with children can relate to that. 'It's just a phase

180

that kids go through,' some say. Well, I hope (he'll/she'll) outgrow it soon!

"Seriously, though, I love my (son/daughter) and it really was a pleasure watching (name) grow up. I've watched (him/her) grow into a wonderful, caring person — intelligent, kind, loving and with a great sense of humor. And I am so very, very glad that (he/she) met (name), a likewise wonderful, caring person. You have each found the perfect partner, and I am sincerely happy for the both of you.

"I am especially happy that (name) has married my (son/daughter), and I ask you all to raise a glass to (him/her) because I am very proud of (other partners' name). Happy to welcome (him/her) into the family, and I especially thank (him/her) for marrying (name) . . . because (other partners' name), (he/she) is *your problem* now!"

. . .

"If you wrote a poem about your new (husband/wife), I think it might be something like this: 'Dreams do come true/ I found mine in you. / In the glow of your eyes/ So worldly and wise;/ In the way that you smile,/ Honest, no guile;/ In the way that you speak/ softly, unique/ When you whisper your Love for me./

"Dreams do come true/I found mine in you./ In a touch tender, but strong/ I lose myself in your arms;/ In lips soft and kissable/ I become Loves disciple./ In the beat of your heart/ When it echoes *my* heart and/ Whispers your Love for me.'

181

"And my sincere wish for you both is that you *always* hear that whisper of Love!"

. . .

"I speak from experience: the Honeymoon is never over! It may seem to be, with the constant drudge of daily life; with work ['and school', 'and the kids' – if appropriate] and the small things that chip away at its foundations. But, trust me, the Honeymoon is never over! It constantly rebuilds itself, comes back into being; every time you think about each other and the Love you share, and every time you remember this wonderful day! So while it seems that everything that has a beginning must have an end, trust me, just remember the Love you share today and you'll indeed find that the Honeymoon is never over!"

. . .

Dear Reader, if you will allow me a personal reminiscence—My Father's advice to me at my wedding:

"Everyone will want to give you advice on married life. Some of it may even be true! But trust me, son, there is only one thing you need to know to make your lives together as smooth as silk. Two simple phrases made up of five simple words. It doesn't much matter which of you say them, or whether you are in the right or the wrong when you do so. It only matters that *one of you* say them. What are these five magic words? 'Yes, dear!' and 'I'm sorry, dear!'"

Quotations for Use
And Inspiration

I have chosen a small selection of quotations that are appropriate for use in both speeches and toasts. This brief selection is *not* meant to be definitive. Obviously, these are only a few of the quotations that are available on the subjects of love, marriage, and domestic life. Quotes on these subjects by writers such as Shakespeare or Kahlil Gibran could fill a book by itself! So just because you don't find your favorite quote, poem or song lyric listed here, feel free to use it anyway.

As mentioned previously in the book, many quotes lend themselves to various uses. Apply these quotes as you need to and adjust them to suit your speech. These quotations have echoed across time, and perhaps may inspire you to create some unique quotations of your own!

These select few are only meant to give you a resource base if you do not have the time or inclination to research quotations on your own. Others of you may wish to research *more* quotations by the writers I've included. To that end, I have tried—where possible—to state the source of the quotation so that you may refer to the original work for other quotes.

Please note that because these quotations can be used variously, I have not tried to group them by type (Best Man, Father of the Bride, etc.). Instead, I have listed them alphabetically by author. Also, any errors in spelling or grammar appear in the original.

. . .

Henry Adams (1838-1918) American author/historian

"Everyone who marries goes it blind, more or less."
Esther: A Novel (1884), Ch. VII

. . .

Joseph Addison (1672-1719) English essayist/poet

"Love is like a friendship caught on fire. In the beginning a flame, very pretty, often hot and fierce; but still only light and flickering. As love grows older, our hearts mature and our love becomes as coals, deep-burning and unquenchable." *Cato: A Tragedy* (1713)

"When love's well-timed 'tis not a fault of love." *Ibid.* Act 3 Sc 1

"Loveliest of women! heaven is in thy soul, Beauty and virtue shine forever round thee, Bright'ning each other! thou art all divine!" *Ibid.* Act 3 sc. 2

"Mysterious love, uncertain treasure, Hast thou more of pain or pleasure!" *Rosamond* (c. 1707), Act III, scene 2

"Marriage enlarges the scene of our happiness and miseries. A marriage of love is pleasant; a marriage of interest, easy; and a marriage where both meet, happy. A happy marriage has in it all the pleasures of friendship, all the enjoyments of sense and reason, and, indeed, all the sweets of life." *The Spectator* #261

. . .

Thomas a Kempis (1380-1471) German Christian writer

"Nothing is sweeter than love, nothing more courageous, nothing higher, nothing wider, nothing more pleasant, nothing fuller, and nothing better in heaven or on earth . . ."

From *The Imitation of Christ* (1418) Book 3, chapter 5 "The Wonderful Effect of Divine Love"

"Love is active, sincere, affectionate, pleasant and amiable; courageous, patient, faithful, prudent, long-suffering, resolute, and never self-seeking."

185

"Love feels no burden, thinks nothing of trouble, attempts what is above its strength, pleads no excuse of impossibility; for it thinks all things lawful for itself, and all things possible."

See original quote below:

"Love feels no burden, regards not labors, strives toward more than it attains, argues not of impossibility since it believes that it may and can do all things." *Ibid.* chapter. 6

.   .   .

Aristotle (384 BCE-322 BCE) Greek philosopher

"Love is composed of a single soul inhabiting two bodies." Assertion attributed to Aristotle in *Lives of Eminent Philosophers* by Diogenes Laërtius

.   .   .

St. Augustine (354-430) early Christian theologian

"As love grows within you, so too does beauty grow; for love is the beauty in your soul." *Homilies on the First Epistle of John*, Ninth Homily

"Choose to love whomsoever thou wilt: all else will follow." *On the Mystical Body of Christ*

"This is the very perfection of a man, to find out his own imperfections." To which I add — "and the best way to discover your imperfections is to ask to your spouse!" (JTS)

. . .

Francis Bacon (1561-1630) English writer/philosopher

"It is impossible to love and be wise." Essay *Of Love*

. . .

Honore de Balzac (1799-1850) French novelist

"True love is eternal, infinite, and always like itself. It is equal and pure, without violent demonstrations: it is seen with white hairs and is always young at heart." *Le lys Dans la Vallee* (1836)

"One should believe in marriage as in the immortality of the soul." *Comedie Humaine* (1841)

. . .

Henry Ward Beecher (1813-1887) American clergyman

"Love without faith is as bad as faith without love."

The Original Plymouth Pulpit: Sermons of Henry Ward Beecher in Plymouth Church, Brooklyn, vol. 2 (1893)" Evils of Anxious Forethought" (delivered 9 May 1869)

. . .

Aphra Behn (1640-1689) English dramatist

"Each moment of the happy lover's hour is worth an age of dull and common life." *The Younger Brother* (1696), Act III, section 2

"Love . . . once fled, never returns more." *The History of the Nun* (1688)

. . .

The Bible King James Version (see also the section *Bible Readings* in the Appendices)

Genesis 2:18 "It is not good that man should be alone."

Proverbs 12:4 "A virtuous woman is a crown to her husband"

Proverbs 31:10 "Who can find a virtuous woman? for her price is far above rubies."

Matthew 19:5-6 "Wherefore they are no more twain (two), but one flesh. What therefore God hath joined together, let not man put asunder."

Mark 6:21 (also Luke 12:34) "For where your treasure is, there will your heart be also."

1 John 3:18 "... let us not love in word, neither in tongue; but in deed and in truth."

Ephesians 4:2-3 "With all lowliness and meekness, with longsuffering, forbearing one another in love; Endeavouring to keep the unity of the Spirit in the bond of peace."

188

1 Peter 4: 8 "And above all things have fervent charity (love) among yourselves: for charity (love) shall cover the multitude of sins."

Revelations 21:5 "Behold, I make all things new."

. . .

Ambrose Bierce (1842-1914?) American writer

"Love, noun: A temporary insanity curable by marriage..." *The Devil's Dictionary* (1911)

"Marriage, noun: The state or condition of a community consisting of a master, a mistress, and two slaves, making in all two." (ibid)

. . .

William Blake (1757-1827) English poet/artist

"If a thing loves, it is infinite." *Annotations to Swedenborg* (1788)

"Love seeketh not itself to please,

Nor for itself hath any care,

But for another gives its ease,

And builds a heaven in hell's despair."

"The Clod and the Pebble" *Songs of Experience* (1794)

"Those who restrain desire do so because theirs is weak enough to be restrained." *The Marriage of Heaven and Hell* (1790?)

. . .

Boethius (Anicius Manlius Severinus Boethius) (480-525) Roman philosopher

"Who would give a law to lovers? Love is unto itself a higher law." *De Consolatione Philosophiae (The Consolation of Philosophy)* Book III, section 12, line 47

.   .   .

Elizabeth Barret Browning (1806-1861) English poet

"Who so loves believes the impossible."

"If thou must love me, let it be for nought
Except for love's sake only. Do not say
"I love her for her smile—her look—her way
Of speaking gently,—for a trick of thought
That falls in well with mine, and certes brought
A sense of pleasant ease on such a day"—
For these things in themselves, Beloved, may
Be changed, or change for thee,—and love, so wrought,
May be unwrought so. Neither love me for
Thine own dear pity's wiping my cheeks dry,—
A creature might forget to weep, who bore
Thy comfort long, and lose thy love thereby!
But love me for love's sake, that evermore
Thou may'st love on, through love's eternity."

Sonnets from the Portuguese, No. XIV

"How do I love thee? Let me count the ways.
I love thee to the depth and breadth and height
My soul can reach, when feeling out of sight

190

For the ends of Being and ideal Grace.
I love thee to the level of everyday's
Most quiet need, by sun and candlelight.
I love thee freely, as men strive for Right;
I love thee purely, as they turn from Praise.
I love thee with the passion put to use
In my old griefs, and with my childhood's faith.
I love thee with a love I seemed to lose
With my lost saints,—I love thee with the breath,
Smiles, tears, of all my life!—and, if God choose,
I shall but love thee better after death."

Sonnets from the Portuguese, No. XLIII

. . .

Robert Browning (1812-1889) English poet

"Ah, but a man's reach should exceed his grasp,
Or what's a heaven for?"

"Andrea del Sarto," line 98 *Men and Women* (1855)

"Grow old with me! The best is yet to be."

"Rabbi Ben Ezra" Line 1, *Dramatis Personae* (1864)

. . .

Buddha (Siddhartha Gautama) (563-483 BCE) Indian religious reformer

"You can search throughout the entire universe for someone who is more deserving of your love and affection than you are yourself, and that person is not to be found anywhere. You yourself, as much as anybody in the entire universe deserve your love and affection."

"The only real failure in life is not to be true to the best one knows."

"Thousands of candles can be lit from a single candle, and the life of the candle will not be shortened. Happiness never decreases by being shared." *Sutta Nipata*

. . .

Edmund Burke (1729-1797) Irish author/philosopher

"You cannot plan the future by the past." letter to a Member of the National Assembly (1791)

. . .

Robert Burns (1759-1796) Scottish poet

"To see her is to love her,
And love but her forever;
For nature made her what she is,
And never made anither! (another)"

Bonny Lesley

. . .

Robert Burton (1577-1640) English writer

"No cord or cable can draw so forcibly, or bind so fast, as love can do with a single thread." *The Anatomy of Melancholy* (1621) part III, section 2

. . .

Byron (George Gordon, Lord Byron) (1788-1824) English poet

"Like the measles, love is most dangerous when it comes late in life."

"I have great hopes that we shall love each other all our lives as much as if we had never married at all." *Letter to Annabella Milbanke* (December 5, 1814)

"She was his life...And to his eye, There was but one beloved face on earth, And that was shining on him." *The Dream* (1816) stanza 2

. . .

Calderon (Pedro Calderon de la Barca) (1600-1681) Spanish dramatist/poet

"Love that is not madness is not love." *El Mayor Monstruo Los Zeplos*

. . .

Thomas Carlyle (1795-1881) Scots essayist

"A loving heart is the beginning of all knowledge." *Critical and Miscellaneous Essays* (1827-1855)

"A poet without love were a physical and metaphysical impossibility." (ibid.)

. . .

Philip Dormer Stanhope Chesterfield, 4th Earl Chesterfield (1694-1773) British statesman/writer

"I wish to God that you had as much pleasure in following my advice, as I have in giving it to you." *Letter to his son, 30 August 1749* (first published 1774)

. . .

William Congreve (1670-1729) English playwright/poet

"Eternity was in that moment." *The Old Bachelor* (1693)

. . .

Emily Dickinson (1830-86) American poet

"That love is all there is / Is all we know of love." Poem #1765

. . .

George Eliot (Mary Ann Evans) (1819-1880) English novelist

"Blessed is the influence of one true, loving human soul on another."

"What greater thing is there for two human souls, than to feel that they are joined for life--to strengthen each other in all labor, to rest on each other in all sorrow, to minister to each other in all pain, to be one with each other in silent unspeakable memories at the moment of the last parting?"

Adam Bede (1859) Chapter 54 (?)

. . .

Ralph Waldo Emerson (1803-1882) American writer

"What lies behind you and what lies in front of you, pales in comparison to what lies inside you."

"He who is in love is wise and is becoming wiser, sees newly every time he looks at the object beloved, drawing from it with his eyes and his mind those virtues which it possesses." *Address on the Method of Nature* (1841)

"Perhaps we never saw them before, and never shall meet them again. But we see them exchange a glance, or betray a deep emotion, and we are no longer strangers. We understand them, and take the warmest interest in the development of romance. All mankind love a lover." *Essays: First Series* (1841) "Of Love"

· · ·

Desiderius Erasmus (1466-1536) Dutch philosopher

"There are some people who live in a dream world, and there are some who face reality, and then there are those who turn one into the other."

"For anyone who loves intensely lives not in himself but in the object of his love, and the further he can move out of himself into his love, the happier he is." *Praise of Folly*(1509; printed 1511)

"The chief element of happiness is this: to want to be what you are." *Ibid.*

"Love that has nothing but beauty to keep it in good health is short lived . . ." *Ibid.*

. . .

"They say that love makes you a fool, and **Henry Fielding** [English author, 1707-1754] wrote there is "One fool at least in every marriage." Well, to the wise love of my dear (husband/wife/partner) I play the happiest fool on earth."

. . .

St. Francis of Assisi (Giovanni di Pietro di Bernardone) (1181/82-1226) Catholic friar and founder of the Franciscan religious order

"Lord, make me an instrument of your peace.

"Where this is hatred, let me sow love; Where there is injury, pardon; Where there is doubt, faith; Where there is despair, hope; Where there is darkness, light And where there is sadness, joy.

"O Divine Master, grant that I may not so much seek to be consoled as to console; to be understood as to understand; to be loved as to love. For it is in giving that we receive; it is in pardoning that we are pardoned, and it is in dying that we are born to eternal life."

. . .

Benjamin Franklin (1706-1790) American author, one of the Founding Fathers

"How selfish the being is who does not love. How selfish the being is who is loved yet returns none. How selfish the being is who is loved yet continuously makes it harder to be loved forevermore. If you would be loved, love, and be loveable" Letter by Benjamin Franklin (1706-1790) "If you would be loved ..." Franklin quoted himself from his aphorism in *Poor Richard's Almanack*, which is quoted from Ovid. (see Ovid)

. . .

Thomas Fuller (1608-1661)   English Clergyman

"He knows little that will tell his wife all he knows." *The Good Husband in The Holy State and the Profane State* (1642)

. . .

Thomas Fuller (1654-1734) English physician/writer

"Keep thy eyes wide open before marriage; and half-shut afterward." *Introductio ad Prudentiam, Pt. 2* (1727)

"My son is my son till he have got him a wife, But my daughter's my daughter all the days of her life." Proverb from *Gnomologia* (1732).

"There is more pleasure in loving, than in being loved."

"A woman is good: that is, good for something or good for nothing." *Ibid.*

. . .

Vincent van Gogh (1853-1890) Dutch painter

"Love is something eternal; the aspect may change, but not the essence." Letter from Vincent van Gogh to Theo van Gogh *The Hague, 21-28 March 1883*

"It is good to love many things, for therein lies the true strength, and whosoever loves much performs much, and can accomplish much, and what is done in love, is well done." *The Letters of Vincent van Gogh to his Brother, 1872-1886* (1927) Constable & Co.

. . .

Johann Wolfgang von Goethe (1749-1832) German poet/dramatist

"Love is an ideal thing, marriage a real thing."

"Love can do much, but duty more."

"Love does not dominate; it cultivates." *Das Märchen* (1795)

. . .

Thomas Hardy (1840-1928) English writer

"...warming with currents of revived feeling in perhaps the sweetest of all conditions. New love is the brightest and long love is the greatest. But revived love is the tenderest thing known on earth." *The Hand of Ethelberta* (1875)

. . .

Nathaniel Hawthorne (1804-1864) American novelist

"Love, whether newly-born or aroused from a deathlike slumber, must always create a sunshine, filling the hearts so full of radiance, that it overflows upon the outward world." *The Scarlet Letter* (1850)

. . .

Heinrich Heine (Christian Johann Heinrich Heine) (1797-1856) German poet

On Love: "It is an old story yet remains ever new."

. . .

John Heywood (Fl. 1497-1580) English poet

"A good wife maketh a good husband." *Proverbs* (Something my wife reminds me of constantly! JTS)

. . .

Oliver Wendell Holmes, Sr. (1809-1894) American author

"If a man really loves a woman, of course he wouldn't marry her for the world if he were not quite sure that he was the best person she could possibly marry." *Autocrat of the Breakfast-Table* (1858) Ch. 10

. . .

Homer (ca. 900 BCE) Greek poet

"There's nothing more admirable than two people who see eye to eye keeping house as man and wife, confounding their enemies and delighting their friends." *The Odyssey*

. . .

Elbert Hubbard (1856-1915) American writer

"A friend is someone who knows all about you and loves you just the same."

"Better mend one fault in yourself than a hundred in your neighbor." *An American Bible (1918)*

"The love we give away is the only love we keep." *The Fra: A Journal of Affirmation, Volume 9" (1912)*

"Do not take life too seriously; you'll never get out of it alive." *A Message to Garcia and Thirteen Other Things* (1901)

"Life is just one damn thing after another." *Items of Interest, Volume: 33 (1911)*

"Do your work. Think the good. And evil, which is a negative condition, shall be swallowed up by good. Think no evil; and if you think only good, you will think no evil. Life is a search for power. To have power you must have life, and life in abundance. And life in abundance comes only through great love." *So Here Cometh White Hyacinths: Being a Book of the Heart (1907)*

"I do not read a book; I hold a conversation with the author." The Philistine, a Periodical of Protest – Volume 32 (1910) by Harry Persons Taber, Elbert Hubbard, Society of the Philistines (East Aurora, N.Y.); Page: 176.

. . .

Victor Hugo (1802-1885) French novelist/poet

"To love another person is to see the face of God." *Les Miserables (1862)*

"Love each other dearly always. There is scarcely anything else in the world but that: to love one another." *Ibid.*

"Life's greatest happiness is to be convinced we are loved." *Ibid.*

"To love or have loved, that is enough. Ask nothing further. There is no other pearl to be found in the dark folds of life." *Ibid.*

"You can give without loving, but you can never love without giving. The great acts of love are done by those who are habitually performing small acts of kindness. We pardon to the extent that we love. Love is knowing that even when you are alone, you will never be lonely again. The great happiness of life is the conviction that we are loved. Loved for ourselves and even loved in spite of ourselves." *Ibid.*

"Love is like a tree, it grows of its own accord, it puts down deep roots into our whole being."
Notre-Dame de Paris (1831)

"To put everything in balance is good, to put everything in harmony is better." *"Quatre-vingt-treize* (Ninety-Three) (1874), Book VII, Chapter V

. . .

Samuel Johnson (1709-1784) English writer and lexicographer

"Love is the wisdom of the fool and the folly of the wise." in *James Boswell's Life of Johnson*

Love is "A triumph of hope over experience." *Ibid.*

"Marriage has many pains, but celibacy has no pleasures." *The Prince of Abissinia: A Tale. – Volume 2 (1759); Chapter: XXVI.*

"Marriage is the strictest tie of perpetual friendship, and there can be no friendship without confidence, and no confidence without integrity." "The Rambler" (1750) by Samuel Johnson; No. 18, May 19, 1750

. . .

Julian of Norwich (1342-1413) English Medieval mystic

"Love was without beginning, is, and shall be without ending." *Revelations of Divine Love* (c. 1393), Ch. 22

"Our life is all grounded and rooted in love, and without love, we may not live." *Revelations of Divine Love* (c. 1393), Ch. 48

. . .

John Keats (1795-1821) English poet

"I love you the more in that I believe you had liked me for my own sake and for nothing else." *Letter to Fanny Brawne, July 8, 1819*

"A thing of beauty is a joy forever: Its loveliness increases; it will never Pass into nothingness." *Endymion* (1818) Bk 1, section 1

. . .

Helen Keller (1880-1968) American author/activist

"The best and most beautiful things in the world cannot be seen or even touched. They must be felt with the heart."
The Story of My Life (1905)

. . .

Omar Khayyam (1048-1131) Persian poet

"Ah, Love! could you and I with him conspire
To grasp this sorry Scheme of Things entire
Would we not shatter it to bits—and then
Re-mould it nearer to the Heart's Desire?"

Rubaiyat of Omar Khayyam (1120) Stanza IX. FitzGerald's Translation

. . .

Lao Tzu (ca. 6th Century BCE) Legendary Chinese philosopher

"Being deeply loved by someone gives you strength, while loving someone deeply gives you courage."

"Love is of all passions the strongest, for it attacks simultaneously the head, the heart and the senses." *Ibid.*

"The Tao is like a well: used but never used up. It is like the eternal void: filled with infinite possibilities." *Ibid. Ch.* 4 [change "The Tao" to "Love" and use as paraphrase]

"Knowing others is wisdom, knowing yourself is Enlightenment" *Ibid. Ch.* 33

"Kindness in words creates confidence. Kindness in thinking creates profoundness. Kindness in giving creates love." *Ibid.*

"He who knows does not speak; he who speaks does not know." *Ibid. Ch.* 56 *Tao Te Ching*

. . .

G. E. Lessing (Gotthold Ephraim Lessing) (1729-1781) German writer/dramatist

"Yesterday I loved, today I suffer, tomorrow I die: but I still think fondly...of yesterday." *Lied aus dem Spanischen* (1780)

. . .

Henry Wadsworth Longfellow (1807-1882) American poet

"It is difficult to know at what moment love begins; it is less difficult to know that it has begun." *Kavanagh: A Tale,* (1849) Chapter XXI.

· · ·

Martin Luther (1483-1546) German religious reformer

"There is no more lovely, friendly and charming relationship, communion or company than a good marriage." *Table Talk* (1569) *Tischreden* (1569)

"Let the wife make the husband glad to come home, and let him make her sorry to see him leave."

"You are not only responsible for what you say, but also for what you do not say."

"Who loves not wine, women, and song/Remains a fool his whole life long." *Attributed*

· · ·

George MacDonald (1824-1905) Scots writer/minister

"It is by loving, and not by being loved, that one can come nearest the soul of another; yea, that, where two love, it is the loving of each other, and not the being loved by each other, that originates and perfects and assures their blessedness." *Phantastes* (1858)

· · ·

Michel de Montaigne (1533-1592) French essayist

"A good marriage would be between a blind wife and a deaf husband." *Essais* (1580)

"I quote others only in order the better to express myself." *Ibid.*

"I know that the arms of friendship are long enough to reach from the one end of the world to the other" *Ibid,*

"There is no more expensive thing than a free gift."

"If there is such a thing as a good marriage, it is because it resembles friendship rather than love." *Ibid.*

. . .

Baron Eligius Franz Joseph von Münch-Bellinghausen (1806—1871) Austrian playwright, poet

"Two souls with but a single thought,/Two hearts that beat as one." *Der Sohn der Wildnis* (1842) Act II *Misattributed to John Keats*

. . .

Friedrich Nietzsche (1844-1900) German philosopher

"There is always some madness in love, but there is also always some reason in madness." *Thus Spoke Zarathustra* (1883) *Also attributed to Robert Louis Stevenson*

. . .

Ovid (Publius Ovidius Naso) (43 BCE – 17 CE) Roman poet

"If you want to be loved, be lovable." *Ars Amatoria (The Art of Love)* (ca. 2 CE) Book II, 107

. . .

Blaise Pascal (1623-1662) French philosopher

"The heart has its reasons, which Reason does not know." <u>Pensées</u>, (1670) Section IV On the Means of the Belief

"We arrive at truth, not by reason only, but also by the heart." *Ibid.*

"When one does not love too much, one does not love enough." *Ibid.*

"To understand is to forgive." *Ibid.*

"In difficult times carry something beautiful in your heart." *Ibid.*

"Kind words do not cost much. They never blister the tongue or lips." *Ibid.*

"When we are in love we seem to ourselves quite different from what we were before." *Ibid.*

. . .

Thomas Love Peacock (1785-1866) English writer

Declares that women are:

"The last, best work; the noblest gift of Heaven." *The Vision of Love* in *Palmyra and Other Poems* (1806)

.   .   .

Petrarch (Francesco Petrarca) (1304-1374) Renaissance Italian poet

"Love is the crowning grace of humanity, the holiest right of the soul, the golden link which binds us to duty and truth, the redeeming principle that chiefly reconciles the heart to life, and is prophetic of eternal good."

As quoted in *Notable Thoughts About Women: A Literary Mosaic* (1882) by Maturin Murray Ballou

"To be able to say how much you love is to love but little." *To Laura in Life* (c. 1327-1350), Canzone 37

.   .   .

Plato (428/7 BCE-424/3 BCE) Greek philosopher

"Every heart sings a song, incomplete, until another heart whispers back. Those who wish to sing always find a song. At the touch of love everyone becomes a poet."
The Symposium (385 BCE-370 BCE)

.   .   .

Edgar Allan Poe American author (1809-1849)

"We loved with a love that was more than love." *Annabel Lee* (1849)

. . .

Alexander Pope (1683-1744) English poet

"Is it, in heaven, a crime to love too well?" *Elegy to the Memory of an Unfortunate Lady* (1717)

. . .

Quran (Koran) ayah (verses)

[25:74] "And they say, "Our Lord, let our spouses and children be a source of joy for us, and keep us in the forefront of the righteous."

[30:21] "Among His proofs is that He created for you spouses from among yourselves, in order to have tranquility and contentment with each other, and He placed in your hearts love and care towards your spouses."

. . .

Francois de La Rochefoucauld (1613-1680) French writer

"There is only one kind of love, but there are a thousand different versions." Maxim 74 *Reflections; or Sentences and Moral Maxims* (1665–1678)

"True love is like ghosts, which everyone talks about and few have seen." Maxim 76

"Who lives without folly is not as wise as he thinks." Maxim 209

"In friendship and in love, one is often happier because of what one does not know than what one knows." Maxim 441

.   .   .

Jalal-Uddin Rumi (1207-1273) Persian poet/mystic

"The minute I heard my first love story, I started looking for you, not knowing how blind that was. Lovers don't finally meet somewhere. They're in each other all along."

"Love will find its way through all languages on its own."

"Love rests on no foundation. It is an endless ocean, with no beginning or end."

"This is a gathering of Lovers. In this gathering, there is no high, no low, no smart, no ignorant, no special assembly, no grand discourse, no proper schooling required. There is no master, no disciple. This gathering is more like a drunken party, full of tricksters, fools, mad men and mad women. This is a gathering of Lovers."

"Wherever you are, and whatever you do, be in love."

.   .   .

George Sand (Amantine-Lucile-Aurore Dupin) (1804-1876) French writer

"Don't walk in front of me, I may not follow. Don't walk behind me, I may not lead. There is only one happiness in life, to love and be loved." *Also attributed to Albert Camus*

"There is only one happiness in life, to love and be loved." Letter 1862

. . .

Friedrich Schiller (1759-1805) German poet

"Love is only known by him who hopelessly persists in love." *Don Carlos* (1787)   Act 2 sc. 8

"What is life without the radiance of love?" *Wallenstein* (1798) Act 4 sc. 12

"Who reflects too much will accomplish little" *Wilhelm Tell* (1803) Act 3 sc. 1

. . .

Franz Schubert (1797-1828) Austrian composer

"Happy is the man who finds a true friend, and far happier is he who finds that true friend in his wife"

. . .

Sir Walter Scott (1771-1832) Scots novelist/poet

"True love's the gift which God has given
To man alone beneath the heaven.

It is the secret sympathy,
The silver link, the silken tie,
Which heart to heart, and mind to mind,
In body and in soul can bind."

The Lay of the Last Minstrel (1805), Canto V, Stanza 13

.   .   .

William   Shakespeare   (1564-1616) English play-wright/poet

From the Plays

"Age cannot wither her, nor custom stale her infinite variety." *Antony & Cleopatra* Act2 sc. 2 (1606-07)

"No sooner met but they looked; no sooner looked but they loved; no sooner loved but they sighed; no sooner sighed but they asked one another the reason; no sooner knew the reason but they sought the remedy; and in these degrees have they made a pair of stairs to marriage..." *As You Like It* Act V sc. 2 (1596-1600)

"Doubt thou the stars are fire; doubt the sun doth move; doubt truth be a liar; but never doubt I love." *Hamlet* Act 2 sc. 2 (1599-1600)

"Brevity is the soul of wit." *Ibid.* Act 2 sc. 2

"We know what we are, but know not what we maybe." *Ibid.* Act 4 sc. 5

"God, the best maker of all marriages, Combine your hearts in one." *Henry V* Act I sc. 2 (1598-99)

"Men of few words are the best men." *Ibid.* Act 3 sc. 2

"Love looks not with the eye, but with the mind." *A Midsummer Night's Dream* Act 1 scene 1 (1596)

"The course of true love never did run smooth." *Ibid.* Act 1 sc. 1

"It is a wise father that knows his own child." *The Merchant Of Venice* Act 2 Sc. 2 (1596-97)

"...love is blind, and lovers cannot see the pretty follies that themselves commit." *Ibid.* Act 2 scene 6

"Love looks not with the eyes, but with the mind; And therefore is wing'd cupid painted blind." *The Merry Wives of Windsor* Act 1 sc. 1 (1597-1601?)

"Men should be what they seem." *Othello* Act 3 sc. 3 (1604-05)

"How long a time lies in one little word!" *Richard II* Act 1 sc. 3 (1595-96)

"My bounty is as boundless as the sea, my love as deep; the more I give to thee the more I have, for both are infinite." *Romeo and Juliet* Act 2 sc. 2 (1595-96)

"To be wise, and love, exceeds man's might." *Troilus & Cressida* Act 3 sc. 2 (1597-1602?)

"Words, words, mere words, no matter from the heart." *Ibid.* Act 5 sc. 3

"Love sought is good, but given unsought is better." *Twelfth Night* Act 3 sc. 1 (1599-1600)

From the Poems and Sonnets (1593-1600)

"If I could write the beauty of your eyes, And in fresh numbers number all your graces, The age to come would say, this poet lies, Such heavenly touches ne'er touch'd earthly faces." Sonnet 17

"For thy sweet love remembered such wealth brings that I scorn to change my state with kings." Sonnet 24

"Let me not to the marriage of true minds
Admit impediments. Love is not love
Which alters when it alteration finds,
Or bends with the remover to remove.
Oh no! It is an ever-fixed mark
That looks on tempests and is never shaken.
It is the star to every wandering bark,
Whose worth's unknown, although his height be taken.
Love's not Time's fool, though rosy lips and cheeks
Within his bending sickle's compass come.
Love alters not with his brief hours and weeks,
But bears it out even to the edge of doom.
If this be error and upon me proved,
I never writ, nor no man ever loved." Sonnet 116

. . .

Percy Bysshe Shelley (1792-1822) English poet

"Familiar acts are beautiful through love." [So treasure the "little" things] *Prometheus Unbound*, The Earth, Act 4

. . .

Sophocles (496 BCE-406 BCE) Greek playwright

"One word frees us of all the weight and pain of life: That word is love." *Oedipus at Colonus* (ca. 401BCE) line 1616-18

. . .

Robert Louis Stevenson (1850-1894) Scots novelist/poet

"You can give without loving, but you can never love without giving." *Across the Plains (1892)* see also Victor Hugo

. . .

Rev. Sydney Smith (1771-1845) English churchman

"My definition of marriage...it resembles a pair of shears, so joined that they cannot be separated; often moving in opposite directions, yet always punishing anyone who comes between." Recounted in *Memoir* of Lady Holland Ch. 2

· · ·

Socrates (470 BCE-399 BCE) Greek philosopher

"By all means marry; if you get a good wife, you'll become happy; if you get a bad one, you'll become a philosopher."

· · ·

Anne Louise Germaine de Staël (1766–1817), (Madame de Staël), Swiss author

"Love is a symbol of eternity. It wipes out all sense of time, destroying all memory of a beginning and all fear of an end." *Corinne* (1807), Book VIII, Chapter II.

· · ·

Bayard Taylor (1825-1878) American poet

"I love thee, I love but thee, with a love that shall not die till the sun grows cold and the stars are old, and the leaves of the Judgment Book unfold." in *Bartlett's Familiar Quotations*, 10th ed. (1919)

· · ·

Alfred, Lord Tennyson (1809-1892) English poet

"I will love thee to the death, And out beyond into the dream to come." *Idylls of the King* (1856–1885)

"If I had a flower for every time I thought of you, I could walk in my garden forever." *Locksley Hall* (1835, pub. 1842)

· · ·

Tertullian (Quintus Septimius Florens Tertullianus) (160 -220 CE) early Church writer

"How beautiful, then, the marriage of two Christians, two who are one in home, one in desire, one in the way of life they follow, one in the religion they practice . . . Nothing divides them either in flesh or in spirit . . . They pray together, they worship together, they fast together; instructing one another, encouraging one another, strengthening one another. Side by side they visit God's church and partake God's banquet, side by side they face difficulties and persecution, share their consolations. They have no secrets from one another; they never shun each other's company; they never bring sorrow to each other's hearts . . Seeing this Christ rejoices. To such as these He gives His peace. Where there are two together, there also He is present."

.   .   .

William Makepeace Thackeray (1811-1863) English writer

"It is best to love wisely, no doubt; but to love foolishly is

better than not to be able to love at all." *The History of Pendennis* (1848-1850), Ch. 6.

.   .   .

Henry David Thoreau (1817-1862) American essay-ist/poet

"Love must be as much a light, as it is a flame."

• • •

Mark Twain (Samuel Langhorne Clemens) (1835-1910) American novelist

"Love seems the swiftest, but it is the slowest of all growths. No man or woman really knows what perfect love is until they have been married a quarter of a century." *Mark Twain's Notebook*

". . . to get the full value of joy, you must have someone to divide it with." epigram from *Pudd'nhead Wilson's Calendar* in *Following the Equator* (1897)

• • •

Virgil (Publius Vergilius Maro) (70 BCE-19 BCE) Roman poet

"Now I know what love is." *Eclogues*, Book VIII, line 43. (translated by John Dryden)

"Love conquers all things; let us, too, give into love." *Ibid.* Book X, line 69 .

"...how I saw you! How I fell in love! How an awful madness swept me away!"

"Love begets love, love knows no rules, this is the same for all."

• • •

Voltaire (François-Marie Arouet) (1694-1778) French philosopher

"Each player must accept the cards life deals him or her: but once they are in hand, he or she alone must decide how to play the cards in order to win the game."

"Love is a canvas furnished by Nature and embroidered by imagination."

"The best is the enemy of the good." *La Bégueule* in *Contes* (1772)

.   .   .

Isaac Watts (1674-1748) English hymn writer

"Love is so amazing, so divine, demands my soul, my life, my all." *When I Survey The Wondrous Cross* in *Hymns and Spiritual Songs* (1707)

.   .   .

John Wesley (1703-1791) English clergyman/reformer

"An ounce of love is worth a pound of knowledge." *Letter to Joseph Benson (7 November 1768)*

"Though we cannot think alike, may we not love alike? May we not be of one heart, though we are not of one opinion?" Sermon 39 *Catholic Spirit*

.   .   .

Walt Whitman (1819-1892) American poet

"Be not dishearten'd, affection shall solve the problems of freedom yet,
Those who love each other shall become invincible..."

Leaves of Grass, DRUM-TAPS, Over the Carnage Rose Prophetic a Voice (1860; 1867)

"The strongest and sweetest songs yet remain to be sung." *Leaves of Grass*

Anonymous Quotes

"You don't marry someone you can live with; you marry the person who you cannot live with*out*."

. . .

"Remember that a successful marriage depends on two things: (1) finding the right person and (2) *being* the right person."

. . .

"Marriage is a three ring circus: engagement *ring*, wedding *ring*, and suffe*ring*."

. . .

"Spouse: someone who'll stand by you through all the trouble you wouldn't have had if you'd stayed single."

．　．　．

"It's easy to understand Love at first sight, but how do we explain Love after two people have been looking at each other for years?"

．　．　．

"Married couples who Love each other tell each other a thousand things without talking."--Chinese Proverb

．　．　．

"When I saw you I was afraid to meet you. When I met you I was afraid to kiss you. When I kissed you I was afraid to Love you. Now that I Love you, I am afraid to lose you."

．　．　．

"If I had a rose for every time I thought of you, I'd be picking roses for a lifetime."--Swedish Proverb

．　．　．

"There is a place you can touch a woman that will drive her crazy: Her heart."

．　．　．

"There are three kinds of men who do *not* understand women: the young, the old, and the middle-aged."

. . .

"Love is being stupid together."

. . .

"Love may be blind but marriage is a real eye-opener."

. . .

"Love is like quicksilver (mercury) in the hand. Leave the fingers open and it stays. Clutch it, and it darts away."

. . .

"Love is like a butterfly, it settles upon you when you least expect it."

. . .

"If I know what Love is, it is because of you."

. . .

"Love isn't finding a perfect person; it's seeing an imperfect person perfectly."

. . .

"Before I met you I never knew what it was like to smile for no reason."

. . .

"Love which has been tested by distance and obstacles, and has passed, is true Love."

. . .

"I wrote your name in the sand, but the waves washed it away. I wrote your name in the sky, but the wind blew it away. So, I wrote your name in my heart and that's where it will stay."

. . .

"When you smiled you had my undivided attention. When you laughed you had my urge to laugh with you. When you cried you had my urge to hold you. When you said you loved me, you had my heart forever."

. . .

"Love is a flower which turns into fruit at marriage." – Finnish Proverb

. . .

"I miss you a little, I guess you could say, a little too much, a little too often, and a little more each day."

. . .

"The first to apologize is the bravest. The first to forgive is the strongest. The first to forget is the happiest."

. . .

"True Love never grows old."

. . .

"To the world, you may be one person, but to me, you *are* the world."

. . .

Variant—"To the world, you may be one person, but to one person you may be the world."

. . .

"Love is the only game that is not called on account of darkness."

. . .

"You played 'Love's lotto' and beat the odds."

225

. . .

"Any man can love a hundred different women over time, but only true love lets a man find a hundred ways to love one woman over a lifetime." Paraphrase of the Chinese proverb.

. . .

"Gold, silver, diamonds, pearls; jewelry, money may be precious. But Love is the only true treasure."

. . .

"When their children find true Love, parents find true joy."

. . .

"I have been a wanderer all of my life, but I need not search the world for love, for I find it with you. And I wonder at the wonder that *is* you."

Toasts

This is a short sample of some appropriate toasts with which to end your wedding speech. You no doubt have found others in the book itself. You may choose to rewrite these to include The Couple's names in the toast itself or you may decide to add the following at the end of any of the toasts: "Ladies and Gentlemen! To ____ and ____!"

Note: You may wonder why every toast ends with an exclamation mark. That is simply because every toast *is* an exclamation! Your toast exclaims your best wishes for The Couple! You may also wonder why I have capitalized the "L" in love. It is simply because, in your toast, love is specific to The Couple and personified, making it a proper noun. (Grammarians may argue, but poets won't!)

· · ·

"May the Love you both share this day live always in your hearts."

. . .

"I wish you all the Love in the world, always!"

. . .

"My best wishes for a long, happy life together!"

. . .

"Thank you for allowing me to share this beautiful occasion! I wish you both the beauty of this (day/night) throughout your lives together!"

. . .

"No two people deserve happiness as much as you both do! Happiness always!"

. . .

"God Bless you both. Now and always! Congratulations!"

. . .

"May the joy you find (today/tonight) be yours forever!"

. . .

"May you both understand, forgive, and always Love each other!"

. . .

"The stars have aligned! You are together! May those stars brighten your nights, and your Love the day, as does the sun. May you be always guided by the light in each other's eyes and the light of Love in each other's hearts!"

. . .

"Each couple is special; each Love unique unto itself. Never before have two people Loved as you do. May you always remember that; may you always rejoice in it; may you always Love!"

. . .

"May God (the Lord, the Almighty, etc.) bless you both today and all the days of your lives!"

. . .

"You have found in each other a partner for life. A someone to trust, a someone who cares, a someone who Loves. My wish is that you always remember that and cherish and honor each other, now and forever!"

. . .

"Now life really begins! May you share all that comes with grace and understanding. May you share it with joy. May you share it in the knowledge that you share it *together*. And may you always share it with Love!"

. . .

"Money only pays the bills. It is the golden Love in your hearts that pays for a lifetime together. The silver in your pocket will tarnish over time, but the golden Love within you both will glisten always. As you go through life together, may the Bank of Life always hold the gold in your hearts!"

· · ·

"There are poems to Love and volumes written about it. Yet none can describe what you both feel right now. My wish is that you always remember that feeling, that indescribable joy, that ultimate bliss. May you *never* forget your Love!"

· · ·

"Here's to the both you! May you share joy and Love, always! You deserve each other! And may you come to realize that as the years go by, when you hear someone say, 'Those two? They *deserve* each other!' You will wholeheartedly agree!"

· · ·

"Love is weird mathematics! "One" becomes "Two" and the "Two" join as "One". I don't understand it. But then again, I was never any good at math; so my Best Wishes to you both. You *added* Love to your lives and *subtracted* loneliness. I pray you never *divide* and I hope that soon you two *multiply*!"

. . .

"A toast to the Bride and Groom/ 'Cause before too soon/ They'll leave the room/ To start their Honeymoon!"

. . .

"May the joy and Love you find today be yours always (forever)!"

. . .

"I simply wish you to always look *to* each other to find Love, and when you look *at* each other, to always find Love!"

. . .

"My wish is that you accept all our blessings tonight and God's (the Lord's, the Almighty's, etc.) blessings always! For each day you live in Love *is* a blessing!"

. . .

[As I always sign my Holiday cards, JTS] "I wish you Long Life, Good Health, God's Blessings, and Love, Always!"

. . .

[A bachelor's toast] "I'm honored to be here tonight/ To see you both in wedded bliss!/ To see your joyous wedding/ And see true lover's kiss!/ But I am in no hurry/ To join you in the ranks/ Though I see the love you share tonight/ I have to say 'No thanks!'/ I'm happy as a single man/ And happy to remain so./ I stay out late and drink 'til dawn—/ I've wild oats yet to sow!/ Still, I wish you both the very best:/ Love, happiness, and fun!/ Yes, I see you two, you married types/ And prefer to *see* than *be* one!"

. . .

"I know you're anxious to start your life together. So go with our blessings; go with our Best Wishes; go with the Love of each of us here, but mostly, *just go!*"

• • •

"I wish you all the joy your hearts can hold/ I wish you health as you both grow old,/ I wish your streets are paved with gold!/ I wish you happiness a thousand-fold/ I wish you the sun, the moon and the stars above/ But mostly, I wish you, Love!"

• • •

"Love is where you find it/ And you've found it in each other/ May the Devil never tempt you/ To find it in some other!" **Note**: Sometimes I write the third line as: "May you ne'er be tempted/"

• • •

"Let us raise a glass/ To wish them joy!/ And may what trouble comes/ Be a little girl or boy!"

• • •

"Thank you for allowing me to share this very special moment, and for giving me the chance to wish you both a long life together, and that you both be ever in Love!"

• • •

[From a married person] "Though each marriage is truly one of a kind/There is one common thing that all marriages bind;/That holds them together from the very start/Though time and condition would tear them apart./And all who've been married know what I speak of;/What binds you together today and forever/ Is Love."

. . .

"I think I can speak for everyone here because their best wishes and hopes are the same ones I also hope and wish for you both: Long Life; Good Health; God's Blessings and Love!"

About the Author

For over forty years, J. Thomas Steele has helped countless Brides, Grooms, and members of the wedding party write both vows and wedding speeches. His son's engagement encouraged him to "help others help themselves" by writing this book and the others in *The Wedding Series.*

Mr. Steele has an eclectic range of interests, from history and philosophy to food and children's stories, and hopes to share this enthusiasm for both learning and a good tale with his readers. He lives in South Florida and writes both fiction and non-fiction.

Other books in **The Wedding Series**:

On premarital preparation: *Questions for Couples: What to Ask Before You Say "I Do": A Primer for Planning Your Future Together and A Guide to What to Expect From Premarital Counseling*

236

On choosing bridesmaids and groomsmen: *The Bride's Guide to the Wedding Party: Choosing—and Using— your Bridesmaids, Groomsmen, and Others to Make YOUR Wedding a Success*

On writing your vows: *The Tao of the Vow: The Path to YOUR Perfect Vows – How to Write and Deliver YOUR Wedding Vows*

On writing and delivering, The Couple's wedding speech: *YOUR Wedding Speech Made Easy: The "How-to" Guide for The Couple (Writing and Delivering YOUR Perfect Wedding Speech)*

For more information about J. Thomas Steele, please visit his author page on Amazon's Author Central page at: amazon.com/author/jthomassteele

Like him on Facebook at: www.facebook.com/jthomassteele.author

<u>Notes</u>

<u>Notes</u>

Notes

Made in the USA
Las Vegas, NV
24 August 2023